The Marriage App
unlocking the irony of intimacy

Praise for *The Marriage App*

Ever thought your marriage could be wonderful if only your spouse would change? In *The Marriage App*, you'll learn that if you love sacrificially, you'll experience greater joy yourself and as a couple. By giving the "irony of intimacy" a chance, your marriage can be transformed.

Jim Daly, President, Focus on the Family

Paul and Virginia were instrumental in the growth we experienced before we got married, and they continue to encourage our marriage to this day. Their understanding of what makes a marriage work has helped us deal with many obstacles. They are extremely caring people, who have shown that having a relationship with Christ is the only way to a successful marriage. They have been such a great example in our lives that we had Paul marry us in June 2012. We trust that the truths from scripture in *The Marriage App* will benefit you as much as the truths are affecting our marriage.

Wes and Anna Welker, newlyweds and NFL All-Pro receiver

The Marriage App is like a healthy piece of cake. It's fun to read (tastes great!) but also has great depth (nutritionally filling!). I'm not sure how the Friesens pulled it off, but it's a spectacular success and a pleasure to recommend.

Gary Thomas, author of *Sacred Marriage* and *The Sacred Search*

We speak from experience that Paul and Virginia Friesen have influenced our relationship in some of our most critical times during our marriage and career in the NFL.

After reading *The Marriage App*, we realize that we are not alone in our struggles and our issues are actually quite common. *The Marriage App* addresses common hardships of marriage and applies practical principles based on the greatest love letter of all time, God's word.

Corey Lynch, NFL defensive back
Cissie Graham Lynch, Special Projects Producer,
    Samaritan's Purse, Billy Graham Evangelistic Association

People want to love and to be loved. Why should something so simple be so difficult? Drs. Paul and Virginia Friesen brilliantly unpack how getting the love we want in marriage will never come from believing the myth "To your own self be true." With characteristic wisdom, wit, and insight, they reveal that the love we hunger for can only be found by encountering Christ's love for us—and following His example of sacrificial love that puts the needs of others ahead of our own. This is a brilliant, insightful book on marriage by two of our leading authorities in the area of family ministry. I cannot recommend it more highly.

Rebecca Manley Pippert, speaker, evangelist, and author of
Out of the Saltshaker

This book is an essential tool for every marriage. Throughout the book, I sensed Paul and Virginia serving as marriage coaches for me, encouraging me, equipping me, and giving me a game plan for a winning marriage that honors God. The chapters are practical, saturated with God's word, and speak right to where I am in my marriage. Whether you've been married 20 years or are engaged, this book will be a cherished companion for the life of your marriage. I honestly wish every couple in our church could have a copy!

Gary Gaddini, Lead Pastor, Peninsula Covenant Church,
Redwood City, California

Having known and worked with Drs. Paul and Virginia Friesen over the last 10 years, I can't think of a better couple to write on the subject of marriage. No matter what state you find your marriage in, you will be giving a gift to your spouse (and yourself!) by reading *The Marriage App.*

Danny Oertli, Parker, Colorado; musician, songwriter, and author
of *Mommy Paints the Sky*

Since our days with the New England Patriots, we have been blessed by Paul and Virginia through their mentoring and teaching. For the many who do not have such a personal opportunity, we strongly encourage you to be "mentored" by them through what they share in *The Marriage App.* Our lives are better and our marriage is stronger because of seeing God's design for our marriage more clearly. We truly believe your marriage will benefit and thrive from these truths.

Benjamin Watson, NFL tight end
Kirsten Watson, Vice President, "One More" Foundation

Most unhealthy marriages don't decay overnight. They crumble incrementally over time, and usually from the inside out. Our unexpressed expectations go unmet, resentment turns to bitterness, and the toxicity grows. Many have counseled on how best to repel or reverse the process, but few have succeeded in helping real people with real marriages like Paul and Virginia Friesen. *The Marriage App* brings solid, biblically-based counsel that can both maintain a great marriage and help those struggling to repair their relationship. And unlike so many authors on the subject, Paul and Virginia speak plainly, address vital concepts directly, and have fun along the way.

David W. Hegg, Senior Pastor, Grace Baptist Church,
Santa Clarita, California; author of *The Obedience Option*

My wife and I both came from difficult family backgrounds. After marriage, we determined to no longer accept broken relationships, dysfunction, and infidelity; instead, we made a covenant to become the first generational legacy builders, starting with a strong, faith-based relationship that would set the tone for our children.

The Friesens not only modeled the level of commitment and faithfulness it was going to take for us to keep our covenant, but they also displayed the fruit that comes from faithfulness to God's plan for marriage. Much of what we have seen and learned from them since 2003 is instilled in *The Marriage App: Unlocking the Irony of Intimacy*. We are confident that the truths from scripture shared in these pages will instruct you and encourage you as well.

Don Davis, veteran NFL player, New England Patriots Super Bowl
Champion, Director of NFL Programs for Pro Athletes Outreach

In *The Marriage App*, Drs. Paul and Virginia Friesen speak in one clear voice, offering a vivid alternative to the unclear noise and cultural confusion of the last 40 years. In a real way, this book challenges its readers to embrace the future hope of their marriages by offering ancient truths for today.

The book boldly examines the concept of "one who is like you, but opposite" when dealing with the differences between men and women within marriage. The Friesens communicate as if they are sitting across from you at your kitchen table with a cup of coffee in hand: softly, tenderly, and with strength. They talk with you, not at you.

The Friesens provide practical parables for today of marriage, clearly demonstrating how loving sacrificially is the route to enjoying intimacy in marriage. Enjoy the journey.

Dennis Mansfield, Boise, Idaho; author of *Beautiful Nate*

I just finished reading *The Marriage App: Unlocking the Irony of Intimacy* and could not put it down. It was like being at one of the Friesens' marriage seminars, but less crowded. :) This is a good book for men, as it makes perfect sense, stays on point, and is easy to follow. The way Paul and Virginia weave the stories of their past into the lessons of marriage are so interesting it keeps you reading without realizing it.

Ken Gaudet, Upton, Massachusetts; husband and father

The Marriage App
unlocking the irony of intimacy

Dr. Paul Friesen
Dr. Virginia Friesen

Home Improvement Ministries
Bedford, MA

THE MARRIAGE APP: Unlocking the Irony of Intimacy
Copyright © 2013 by Paul and Virginia Friesen

Cover design: Elisabeth Hasselbeck, Ginny Townsend, Kris Gonzales
Book design and production: Barbara Steele
Copy editing: Guy Steele

ISBN: 978-1-936907-05-2

Published by HOME IMPROVEMENT MINISTRIES.
For information on other H.I.M. resources, please contact:
    HOME IMPROVEMENT MINISTRIES
    213 Burlington Road, Suite 101-B
    Bedford, MA 01730
E-mail inquiries: info@HIMweb.org
Website: www.HIMweb.org

Printed in the United States of America.   4/13TPS4000

Acknowledgments

Someone once asked us how long it took to write this book. We don't know exactly, but at least 37 years. Our names have been given as the authors, but countless individuals and couples have contributed to the information we are sharing in these pages.

First, we owe a great deal of who we are and what we teach to our parents, who modeled what it means to be faithful to the Lord and to each other in marriage.

We also owe a great deal of gratitude to our many mentors whom we have been privileged to learn from and call friends: John and Grace Tebay, Gordon and Gail MacDonald, Ray and Jan Pendleton, Howard and Cathy Clark, Ray and Carol Johnston, John and Marilyn Nugent, Bob and Carol Kraning, Norm and Winnie Wakefield, and David and Cherylyn Hegg. You have all loved us well and contributed to our growth as a couple and as communicators of the Gospel.

The writings of our friend Gary Thomas, especially *Sacred Marriage*, have been true gifts. Although we have never met, Tim Keller has also mentored us through his writings, especially *The Meaning of Marriage*. We praise God for your faithfulness to God, His word, and your marriages.

We are humbled by those that God has allowed us to intersect with over the years whose stories are told in this book. Your names are in the book, many changed. Thank you for seeking God's heart and discovering the Irony of Intimacy.

For all of our married lives, we have been supported emotionally, spiritually, relationally, and financially by a large number of people who have sacrificially supported us so that we are able to do what we believe God has called us to. Most recently the "Home Improvement Ministries Family" has loved and supported us in ways we will never be able to repay. Your stories have made us laugh, cry, and most importantly see God's power to conform us more to His image and help us grow in honoring Him and each other more fully.

For the last 10 years we have been supported, directed, cared for, and loved by our Home Improvement Ministries Board. Thank you

Guy and Barbara Steele, Richard and Kit Hendricks, Doug and Julie Macrae, Carl and Cathy Blatchley, Ryan and Kelly Plosker, Seth and Melanie Bilazarian, Jack and Leiann Harvey, Dan and Susan Yardley, R.J. and Mary Matthews, John and Marilyn Nugent, and Scott and Sally Shaull.

Special thanks to Guy and Barbara Steele, who have edited every word of this manuscript, read it many times, and given excellent suggestions and comments. We will ever be indebted to you.

To Ginny Townsend, thanks for your creative input and hours on the cover. Thanks for your patience and helpful insights and creativity.

To Gabriel Garcia, thanks for your ideas and wonderful insights in every chapter. This book is much richer because of you. The fact that you are our son-in-law makes us even more grateful.

We appreciate the encouragement many have given us along the way, but especially want to thank those who have read and commented on the manuscript: Ken and Amy Gaudet, Kristin and Bill Smith, Wai and Elaine Wong, Bill and Linda Tiffan, Paul Carroll, and Don and Betsy Hasselbeck. Your comments have helped shape the final outcome in significant ways.

Special thanks to Elisabeth Hasselbeck, who took special interest in the manuscript, agreed to write the foreword, and has a deep heart for sharing the good news of God's design for marriage, especially with those who have previously not explored His design.

We are most thankful for our adult children, Kari, Lisa, and Julie, who have chosen to give their lives fully to Christ. There is no greater gift you could give us. We are grateful that God has brought Gabe to Kari and Derek to Julie to be their lifelong partners in marriage and ministry. We could not be more thankful for the sons-in-law you are. We thank all of you for your input and encouragement in the process of writing this book. We love you all dearly and are thankful for each moment we have together.

Finally, we thank our Heavenly Father who has graciously given us all things, first and foremost His Son, and given us a purpose in living. If any good comes out of this book, we are completely aware that it is because of His great love for us and the work of His Spirit to take these words and use them in the lives of those who choose to read these pages.

To Mel and Helen Friesen
and
To RADM and Mrs. Frank Collins Jr., USN Retired

*You have modeled sacrificial love for each other, and we,
your children, are the beneficiaries of it. Thank you for
your example to us and the rich heritage you have given us.*

To John and Grace Tebay

*You counseled us, married us, and have been our
lifelong mentors and friends. Your legacy of love for each other,
your family, and the body of Christ will never be realized
until we all gather together in eternity.*

Contents

Foreword

Paul and Virginia Friesen, fundamentally grounded in Christ, have thoughtfully represented both sides of the aisle in creating *The Marriage App*, a practical, APPlicable handbook for anyone who wants to get married, be married, and stay married.

Though the concepts are timeless in nature, *The Marriage App* has arrived in a most timely manner. Presently, with every marriage staring down a near 50% failure rate, we have to battle to guard our relationships. The popular solution for a struggling marriage is to end it—despite the cost of obtaining a divorce, legal fees, settlements, and the intangible price that families pay both emotionally and psychologically. Unhappy marriages are no longer . . . "longer". Separation is the new restoration.

Common sense tells us that relationships do not stand still. They are moving in either one direction (intimacy) or the other (separation). Within each moment, a choice is presented—to move either toward or away from one another, and ultimately, God's plan for us to be a united front.

Even for some that may have already read what the Bible says about unconditional love, forgiveness, and being a good spouse, when it comes to proactively applying those principles to our relationship, we let the battery drain out rather than charge. Being "out of sync" with our husband or wife does seem strange in an age where we are constantly prompted to:

Update our phones
Update our iTunes
Update our status
Update our Instagram
Update our profile pics.

It is an embarrassing truth that we are at times more attentive to the number of "likes" we have on Facebook and Instagram than to how much we have "loved" our spouse—and, that we abundantly "share" what we like on social media, yet find it difficult to recall the last intimate detail shared with our husband or wife.

The "low battery" signal that pops up on my iPhone is, in my mind, the equivalent to an oxygen tank running low on a deep sea dive excursion (this remains one of my worst fears, and therefore I have never wanted to even try it!). I actually carry an extra battery or charger in an effort to avoid such a catastrophic disconnect. I know that I am not alone. How can we so desperately fear a technological freeze, yet—at the same time—remain in denial or stagnant in a marital shutdown?

Truth be told, I love my iPhone. I always say that the Bible changed my life, and the iPhone changed my day! It allows me to connect and to work from the car, and my kids' pictures are available to me all day long. I can FaceTime my husband, Tim. It allows me to get news, information, biblical scriptures, music, the weather, my NCAA bracket updates . . . the list goes on.

I (now) take great care of my phone (details to follow). All of this care for something that has offered many things—but really promised me nothing. For as much as I love this particular iPhone, it is all but guaranteed that a newer, faster, better looking iPhone is likely to outshine it within the next 12–24 months.

On the contrary: there is *no* guarantee, nor is it God's plan, that when the person you married seems "outdated" the iWife3 or iHusband4 will be available to you once you trade in your iCurrentlyCan'tStandMySpouse2! Despite our knowing this, our marriage is the precious good that we too often choose not to maintain.

Confession: My attentiveness to my technology has not always come naturally. A year ago, I never synced my phone. I rarely updated my computer. Laziness, good intentions gone bad, and a decision to not *do* the upkeep on my tech were all to blame.

Then came the day. You have had one like it, I suspect: 133 photos and videos on my iPhone—vanished. Precious smiling faces of my three babies, including Christmas morning videos, *gone.* No mater how many restarts, and swipes, and settings I frantically attempted, they would not be retrieved.

Within 17 minutes I was nearly breaking through the glass doors of the Apple Store. One would have thought I was rushing to the emergency room. I was going to fight hard to get back what I had lost, and I was wasting no time doing it. Every minute was too long to let it all somehow escape my reach. How could I ever let something so special just get wiped out? How could I have not backed up my memory? Why did I not take the time it took to simply sync?

Seventeen minutes were all that I let stand between me and the potential loss of my digital life.

And yet years go by before we realize all that we have lost—or stand to lose—in a marriage that has gotten way out of sync.

One is technological; one is biblical. Both require a decision to change it. Both require a practical instruction put into practice. Both have a real consequence if the "I do" becomes . . .

"I DON'T."

The Marriage App offers a multitude of ways by which the principle of intimacy actually becomes the result of the practice. By doing, you become, and by becoming you want to keep doing. This "app" is loaded with techniques that work, founded in over 30 years of couples counseling experience, and offers wise reminders throughout the chapters.

One of my favorites, found in the title of Chapter 4, reads "Realize the enemy is not your spouse." Brilliantly conveyed, the chapter points out that. The real opponent is not the person that said "I do" to you. The real enemy is *evil.* Evil is in hot pursuit and will use everything imaginable to hunt, seek, and destroy your marriage because Love is the *prime* enemy of Satan. Evil does not want you to read this book. Evil definitely does not want you and your husband or wife to read it together, as doing so will only strengthen the very system it wishes to throw into chaos. Evil wants your marriage to fail. Every day, every moment, it is attacking. Evil's goal, simply put, is to have you think that being apart from your spouse is good, despite that we were created to be together. Evil's game plan includes making you think that you are better off forfeiting your marriage, for something that seems better, easier, and less work. Evil is counting on you to give up. I firmly believe that when you put into action the APPlications the Friesens wisely offer, the only way your marriage will end is in *victory*.

Welcome to *The Marriage App*.

Now go on . . .

Unlock. Sync. Charge. Update. Restore.

Elisabeth Hasselbeck

Introduction

You are holding *The Marriage App*. Apps neither easily nor automatically solve issues, but they do give us access to information and tools to help us realize our goals. You might download an app for organizing your calendar, but unless you follow the prompts and input the information, that calendar app is useless. This book is not titled *The Marriage App* because it will automatically give anyone a wonderful marriage. (Wouldn't it be great if all we needed to do was push a button and have that accomplished?) Rather, we call it *The Marriage App* because it offers tools to experience what we all long for in marriage. We do believe, after 37 years of marriage and over 30 years of counseling couples, that God's word is itself the ultimate marriage app. The principles we describe in this book come from scripture and, we believe, are able to unlock the irony of intimacy that all of us long for but often find elusive.

We believe we were all created by God to experience intimacy in life, and the fullest human expression of that in marriage. God actually is the one who thought up marriage, and therefore it makes sense that the principles He writes about in scripture should enable us to experience what we long for and were designed for.

It is no secret that pursuing our own agendas has not accomplished the happiness we have longed for. We trust that as you explore this book you will be open to a counter-intuitive approach to marriage. We believe that as you follow the principles laid out in this book, you will discover the irony of intimacy and experience true joy and fulfillment in your marriage relationship.

As you read *The Marriage App*, you will note that although the book is authored by both of us, it is written using the first person singular ("I" rather than "we"), for reading ease. Please be assured that although Paul is the "voice" of the book, it has come out of our 37 years of living and working together.

So, enjoy the process of learning how loving sacrificially is the route to experiencing intimacy in marriage.

Enjoy the journey—

Paul and Virginia Friesen
May 2013

P. S. *The Marriage App* is designed to stand alone as a book, be used by a couple, and/or be used as a small group discussion guide. However you choose to use it, let it give you added encouragement as you live out this great idea of God's called marriage. For further input and conversation starters, go to the iTunes App store and look for "The Marriage App".

 Care for the one you love

*Be imitators of God, therefore, as dearly loved
children and live a life of love, just as Christ loved
us and gave himself up for us as a fragrant offering and sacrifice to God.   —Ephesians 5:1–2*

*I*t was John and Wendy's favorite vacation spot during
their 38-year marriage: twice each year they would fly
to Hawaii and rent a cottage or stay in a timeshare, sometimes
alone, but often with their family. The islands held many memories for them of a life well spent, a close family, and a sweet marriage. But after a 17-year battle with cancer, John lost his earthly
struggle and entered his heavenly rest. Wendy had asked us to
accompany her on her first return visit to Hawaii after John's
death. We were having lunch out on the balcony overlooking the
Pacific when Wendy started to cry. Assuming she was recalling
some special time on the island with John, we gently asked her,
"What is it, Wendy?" She blurted out, "I wish I'd made him more
Jell-O!"

Wendy then told us, through laughter and tears, that John loved
Jell-O. From the earliest days of their marriage, John always was
asking her to make him Jell-O. She didn't like Jell-O herself and
declined to make it most of the time, claiming it was all empty

calories, nothing but sugar and colored dyes. But now, looking back, she mused, "Why didn't I just give him Jell-O?" As we continued to talk, she said, "The real reason was not all the nutritional stuff, but just that I plain didn't want to make him Jell-O. I didn't like it. But what a simple thing for me to do to bring him a little extra joy for the day. I wish I had made him more Jell-O."

Fortunately, in John and Wendy's case, there were not a lot of other "Jell-O" areas. Unfortunately, for many couples, the accumulation of "Jell-O" moments—not caring about our spouse's needs and desires—culminates in individuals not feeling cared for and loved. In too many cases those marriages end in divorce, or continue in a silent state of contempt and miss out on the joy of intimacy in marriage.

Why do we long for an intimate relationship with our spouse but find it so difficult to experience? Why do we find it so easy to focus on our own desires and preferences over the desires and preferences of our spouse? Why did God make us so different from each other, with difference preferences and desires, if He wanted us to get along? Why didn't He make it easier to love my spouse? Why do so many married couples find it difficult to find true contentment and joy? Though these questions often plague each of us, it is my deep conviction that we truly are designed to be at our best when we put our spouse's needs above our own. The irony is that when we do, we actually find the intimacy we have been longing for.

IN SEARCH OF INTIMACY

What does marital intimacy look like? In its simplest form, intimacy is being fully known and fully loved by another. Don't we all long for such a relationship of acceptance and love? No matter where your marriage is, I imagine you would like to experience more romance, friendship, sexual expression, emotional connection, fun, and a safe environment to grow into all God created you to be. For many, however, this sort of an intimate relationship seems elusive. Sadly, because many have not found intimacy in marriage, they have instead pursued personal "happiness" outside of their marriage.

It is interesting that although we live in a time of the history of the world where we have never had more, we seem to be enjoying life less. The pursuit of individual happiness seems to be at an all-time high. Individuals are pouring their time and money into fulfilling their personal desires and yet are not experiencing the happiness they are seeking. We

> *In its simplest form, intimacy is being fully known and fully loved by another.*

are surrounded by a culture that says "Take care of yourself—no one else will." "You deserve a break today." "Find yourself." "Be true to yourself." "Realize your potential."

In the 80's we bought the ill-founded "self-esteem" program. "Tell your children they are the best, they never lose, they are special, they are the center of the universe." But instead of building self-confidence, we seem to have fed a narcissistic entitlement culture.

I remember reading about a "turbulent 60's" poster, described in a book by Steve Farrar[1]: the iconic beautiful girl with long blonde hair and a flowing gown was running barefoot through a field. Running toward her was a man, also with long flowing hair. The caption read, "You do your thing, and I'll do mine. And if by chance we find each other, it's beautiful." Farrar rightly observed that the caption should have read, "You be selfish, and I'll be selfish, and if by chance we find each other, it's nuclear war." Never has there been a time when more individuals who both believe they are the center of the universe are marrying each other and discovering: it ain't a wonderful life. We have seen a huge spike in the number of couples coming to see us who are ready to call it quits on marriage after only one or two years. Why? Because Miss "It's all about me" has married Mr. "It's all about me"—and they find it's not!

> *Unless the heart is changed, true intimacy cannot be realized.*

The dilemma that couples are finding themselves in is an unmet deep desire for intimacy, which was God's design from the beginning. Adam and Eve were "naked" before each other in every sense of the word: fully known and fully loved, without any shame.

> *The man and his wife were both naked, and they felt no shame.* —Genesis 2:25

At the end of the day, isn't this what each of us long for? A relationship in which we do not need to hide or pretend, and yet are also loved fully. The dilemma we find ourselves in is being wired to desire such intimacy and yet finding it so difficult to experience this intimacy in marriage.

In our search for such intimacy, we read books, listen to podcasts, and go to seminars. We are told we need to date more, get away more, play more tennis together, go to church more. We are told to use such phrases as "When you say that, I feel hurt" instead of "You make me mad." All these suggestions are helpful, but they will never give genuine intimacy. We eventually don't like to do the same things on dates; the vacations come to an end; we lose in tennis; we took the "I" class so know she really meant "you"; we go to church but then come home.

We need less self-help and more reliance on God to transform us into the likeness of Christ. Unless the heart is changed, true intimacy cannot be realized. Only one who reflects the image of Christ will joyfully die to self and instead live for the benefit of his or her spouse. Let's examine how Jesus serves as our ultimate model for sacrificial love.

JESUS, THE PERFECT LOVER

It is easy for some of us that have heard "Jesus stories" all our lives to forget that "lovin' us" was not exactly easy for Jesus. Jesus loved the church even when "the church" rejected him, ridiculed Him, laughed at Him, and finally deserted Him. Jesus' ultimate act of sacrificial love on the cross required His total obedience.

> *And being found in appearance as a man,*
> *he humbled himself*
> *and became obedient to death—*
> *even death on a cross!* —Philippians 2:8

The contemplation of the coming physical torture and the separation from the Father—for the first time in all of eternity—as He descended into Hell caused Him to ask if there were any other way that the salvation of the world could possibly be accomplished.

> *Going a little farther, he fell with his face to the ground and prayed, "My Father, if it is possible, may this cup be taken from me. Yet not as I will, but as you will."* —Matthew 26:39

Contrary to popular belief, Jesus was not singing "It's a happy day and I praise God for the weather . . ." Yes, it was a great and wonderful day, but it was a day of great sacrifice, because that is what love does.

It is with this example of sacrificial love that the Apostle Paul challenges us to love one another with this same love:

Each of you should look not only to your own interests, but also to the interests of others.

Your attitude should be the same as that of Christ Jesus:
Who, being in very nature God,
did not consider equality with God something to be grasped,
but made himself nothing,
taking the very nature of a servant,
being made in human likeness.
And being found in appearance as a man,
he humbled himself
and became obedient to death—
even death on a cross!   *—Philippians 2:4–8*

US, THE IMPERFECT LOVERS

As one of my friends once said, "Dying for my spouse, sure. Living for her, now that's much more difficult." And it is! Since sin entered the Garden of Eden, our propensity is to look out for ourselves before anyone else. God has made provision for us to become one again with our spouse and to get "back

Individualism and isolationism have always been Satan's tactics for destroying marriages.

to the garden," but our selfishness often stands in the way.

From the beginning of time, Satan has been enticing married persons to pursue their own individual goals, desires, needs, and happiness. Individualism and isolationism have always been Satan's tactics for destroying marriages. He *hates* the two becoming one, because that is God's design. In the Garden of Eden, Satan strategically approached Eve alone, not Adam and Eve together.

Satan continues with this same strategy today, doing all he can to isolate couples from each other.

> *Now the serpent was more crafty than any of the wild animals the Lord God had made. He said to the woman, "Did God really say, 'You must not eat from any tree in the garden'?"*
>
> *The woman said to the serpent, "We may eat fruit from the trees in the garden, but God did say, 'You must not eat fruit from the tree that is in the middle of the garden, and you must not touch it, or you will die.'"*
>
> *"You will not surely die," the serpent said to the woman. "For God knows that when you eat of it your eyes will be opened, and you will be like God, knowing good and evil."*
>
> *When the woman saw that the fruit of the tree was good for food and pleasing to the eye, and also desirable for gaining wisdom, she took some and ate it. She also gave some to her husband, who was with her, and he ate it.* —Genesis 3:1–6

It is interesting that the reason Eve was created was that it was not good for Adam to be alone. If God does not want us alone, then Satan will do all he can to have us be alone. Is this starting to make sense? Satan tempts Eve alone and offers her personal experiences alone that are apart from God's design. Adam, who is physically present and should have been protecting her, is also "alone" in his own world and does not interact with her but is oblivious to the catastrophic event taking place right in front of him.

ALONE AGAIN

Recently, while visiting friends, we accompanied them as they picked up their children from school. Before we could turn around, each child was focused on his Game Boy, listening to her iPod, or texting his friend. No one interacted; they were all alone, and it was not good.

Many modern marriages function in much the same way. Each of us is hooked up, tuned out, pursuing our own hobbies and interests—and then wondering why we are not "one" with our spouse.

In Matthew 19, when Jesus is questioned about marriage, He says, "... *the two will become one ... they are no longer two ...*" As much as that flies in the face of today's culture, once we become married we are one. Whatever we pursue as individuals *does* affect our life together, because we are no longer two. From the moment we marry, all decisions must go through the grid of: does this strengthen or weaken our marriage?

> *I do not have a covenant relationship with my dreams; I do with my spouse.*

I am certainly not saying that after marriage each individual no longer has passions, gifts, abilities, hopes and dreams. What I am saying is that after marriage all decisions should treat the marriage relationship as paramount. I may have an opportunity that will fulfill all my individual dreams, but if it takes me away from my covenant partner, I must not pursue that dream. I do not have a covenant relationship with my dreams; I do with my spouse.

The term "covenant" is not used much today. In biblical times, it referred to a lasting commitment that would not change. God established a covenant relationship with the Hebrews, and in that covenant was the security that God would not ever leave them. After the great flood, God set the rainbow in the sky as a reminder of His covenant never to destroy the earth again with a flood.

And God said, "This is the sign of the covenant I am making between me and you and every living creature with you, a covenant for all generations to come: I have set my rainbow in the clouds, and it will be the sign of the covenant between me and the earth. Whenever I bring clouds over the earth and the rainbow appears in the clouds, I will remember my covenant between me and you and all living creatures of every kind. Never again will the waters become a flood to destroy all life. Whenever the rainbow appears in the clouds, I will see it and remember the everlasting covenant between God and all living creatures of every kind on the earth."

So God said to Noah, "This is the sign of the covenant I have established between me and all life on the earth."

—Genesis 9:12–17

So often today when people speak of the marriage covenant, they see it as a negative, something that restricts. This could not be further from the truth. The covenant God made with Noah gives us security that He will always care for us, even when we are not easy to care for. The covenant relationship in marriage, far from being restrictive, should likewise serve as a source of great security and commitment.

LIKE, BUT OPPOSITE

So if this "intimacy and oneness in marriage thing" is so important to God, then why do husbands and wives often seem so opposite from each other? Why did He seem to give us conflicting desires? I mean, He's God, creator of male and female, so why did He make us so different from each other?

In Genesis, after God says it is not good for Adam to be alone, He has all the animals parade in front of Adam. Adam checks them out and names them, but none of them ring his bells. Then God says, "I will make you a suitable helper." In the original language, "suitable helper" literally means "one who is like you, but opposite." So God says: "I want you to get married, become one, and enjoy unity, intimacy, and oneness, so I am going to make you opposites." Is this some kind of a joke? If God wanted Virginia and me to get along better, he should have made her more like me!

Virginia likes order, while I am more "relaxed," shall we say. She loves interacting with people; I tend to like being by myself. She tends to feel there is a "best" way to do life; I just go with the flow. She cuts back on eating when her pants get at all tight; I start cutting back on eating when I can't find any pants that fit. Virginia loves to read; I like to watch TV. Virginia likes

Love can only be fully expressed in marriage through sacrifice.

to balance the checkbook to the penny; I like to do long-term investments . . . and the list goes on.

It was God's idea to make us "like, but opposite," and we'll explore that more fully in Chapter 3. God stated that His creation was "very good," as is recorded after the sixth day of creation. So, simply stated, if something is good from God's perspective, Satan will attempt to jump in and use our "oppositeness" to divide rather than unify. Satan will attempt every way he is able to have each of us focus on our personal desires instead of the desires and interests of our spouse. Satan will attempt to take our differing temperaments and make them as annoying as possible to the other. Satan will attempt to use our different patterns of communication to make us drive each other crazy. He will take sexuality and try to use your differences to drive you to opposite sides of the bed instead of into each other's arms. He will tempt you to live parallel lives, pursuing your own agenda instead of traveling life's highway together.

DIFFERENT IS GOOD

So why did God intentionally, before the fall, make us so different? Why did He seem to make it easy for Satan to use our differences against one another?

I think the answer lies in the fact that God wants us to experience true love, and He knows that without sacrifice we are not able to experience real love. He knows that His love was most fully expressed when He gave His Son, sacrificially, to show His love for us.

"For God so loved the world that he gave his one and only Son, that whoever believes in him shall not perish but have eternal life." —*John 3:16*

SACRIFICIAL LOVE

In the same way, love can only be fully expressed in marriage through sacrifice. Love is knowing your spouse and putting your spouse's interests and desires ahead of your own.

Let me illustrate with a stereotypical example. Suppose I love golf and Virginia hates golf, and I tell her I want to take her golfing to show her how much I love her. No points. Let's say I love golf and she likes it okay. I tell her I am going to show her how much I love her by taking her golfing. Better, but I am still doing what I want to do. If I don't play golf but do go shopping with her? That's love!

During the infatuation stage of a relationship, one may say, "I'm in love"—but those feelings may exist simply because one's needs and desires are being met and the other person makes one happier. In marriage, we best demonstrate our love by meeting the needs of this other person.

Hollywood does a terrific job of portraying the antithesis of true love. In the epic movie *Titanic*, Jack and Rose are said to be truly in love. We know girls who saw that movie five or six times because, they claimed, "It was so romantic." It was *not* romantic; it was a *tragedy*. It did not portray true love. Most likely Jack would have left Rose as soon as they hit port and a more desirable woman came along. Jack did not love Rose; he loved having sex with her three days after meeting her. Love is doing what is best for the one you love—and having sex before marriage is never best.

So: is love simply "doing the right thing?" Is it staying married and being miserable? Is it simply suffering in this life because it's eternity that matters? Not at all! God has a much grander vision of marriage, and so should we.

DESIGNED TO LOVE

We were designed to serve and to sacrificially love. When we do so we are most Christ-like, and thus most alive. There is no better place to be than to be imitating Christ in our relationships. When I think of the older couples I know, it is not the ones that have "looked out for #1" that are fully alive in their old age, it is the ones who have given of themselves to each other. Here is the irony of intimacy: those who have focused on themselves and their personal desires, and feel that if only their mate would change then they could find happiness and intimacy, have missed it. But those who have put their spouse's needs and desires ahead of their own end up experiencing incredible joy themselves, and usually great intimacy as a couple.

DELIGHT IN THE IRONY

One August, we were speaking to a group of coaches in Portland, Oregon. The event was held in a 4-star resort. The setting was spectacular, the food fabulous, and the whole experience designed to get couples "away from it all" so they could be refreshed and renewed. We had finished our third talk of the day, which happened to be on marital intimacy, and were heading to our room around 11 pm when one of the wives in attendance caught us and said she and her husband had just had a big fight. She explained that after our final talk, her husband got up from his chair and with a twinkle in his eye said to her, "Let's go to bed." Without a twinkle in her eye she replied, "No, I really think we need to talk about how our marriage is doing." And the fight began.

We talked to the woman for a while and then all headed to our rooms. About a half hour later—now almost midnight—I had to deliver something to another room and walked through the lobby, only to find the same woman sitting alone reading a book on a couch, while her husband was, no

> *We were designed to serve and to sacrificially love.*

doubt, back in their hotel room. I thought sadly to myself, "Isn't that just like Satan? God gave this couple a weekend away in a 4-star resort with everything they needed to renew their relationship, and Satan throws the 'take care of yourself' card in." No one won—except Satan. The wife wanted to connect relationally and talk about the marriage, the husband wanted to connect physically and make love, and neither of them ended up experiencing what they had desired.

After thinking about the wife alone in the lobby reading a book and the husband fuming in the bedroom, alone, I thought how the night could have ended differently. What if, after saying he wanted to go to bed and hearing her reply that she wanted to talk, he had said, "Sure, we can talk if you wish"? I can almost guarantee that after connecting relationally through conversation, she would have been more interested in physical intimacy. Or, suppose she had said, "Hey, let's go have sex—we can talk tomorrow." He would have been more relational, maybe not that night, but the next day. Do you see? When we sacrificially love and put the interests of our spouse ahead of our own preferences, *we* benefit as well—not manipulatively, but because that is how God designed us to function in marriage.

In the end, it is selfishness that kills marriages—and Christ-like sacrificial service that makes them come alive.

It may be as simple as making more Jell-O, or as complex as changing vocations, but in the end the issue is the same: is our heart set on first pleasing ourselves and looking out for our individual interests, or is it putting the needs, interests, and desires of our spouse ahead of ours? And this is the irony: when we sacrificially love our spouse by putting his or her needs ahead of our own, we both benefit and experience more intimacy.

"For whoever wants to save his life will lose it, but whoever loses his life for me will find it." —Matthew 16:25

In the next chapters we will explore what "making more Jell-O" may look like in your marriage, and how to more fully find this thing called intimacy that we all desire, but often find very elusive.

*W*hen we put our spouse's needs above our own,
not only will they feel loved,
but it will propel our marriage towards greater intimacy.

Reminders

☑ We all desire intimacy.

☑ Most of us find intimacy very elusive.

☑ God's design for us is to not be alone.

☑ Satan wishes to separate and isolate us from each other.

☑ God is the one who created male and female "like, but opposite".

☑ Love is most fully shown through sacrifice.

☑ Satan wants our differences to cause tension rather than bring unity.

☑ It takes discipline to love well.

☑ If we are to love our spouse well, we must know them and sacrificially love them.

☑ When we love our spouse as Christ loved us, we will more fully come alive and be the husband/wife God desires.

☑ When we love our spouse more fully, they in turn will likely love us more fully.

☑ When our spouse loves us more fully, we experience the intimacy we always longed for.

For Couples

Questions

1. Individually write down (or mentally graph) your marriage from the time you were married until the present. On a scale of 1–10 (1 being really miserably married, 10 being "pretty much everything I had hoped for"), how would you say your marriage has been over time? Note especially any significant drops or rises and any patterns you have seen.

2. Now finish this question: I think our marriage would be more satisfying if I _____. (Make sure you list only things *you* could do, not things your spouse could do.)

APPlication

+ Both of you write down what it was that originally attracted you to each other.

+ Go out on a date this month to a place you used to go to or to an activity you used to enjoy together.

+ While together on your date, share your list of what attracted you to each other. (Keep this positive. Don't add "But, boy, have things changed!" or "You never do that anymore." Just focus on what drew you to each other.)

For Groups

1. Each couple share about the first time they met each other.

2. Each person tell what it was about their spouse that first attracted them.

3. What part of the first chapter struck you the most strongly?

4. From your perspective, what is contributing most fully to our disillusionment with marriage today?

5. Read Hebrews 12:1–3 and Hebrews 10:24–25.

   • From these passages, what are some of the things you feel couples could do intentionally that would strengthen their marriage?

   • What do these passages say about the role the church might play in encouraging couples to stay vitally connected and committed to their marriage?

6. How specifically can this group practically encourage each other in this during this study?

Have realistic expectations

Set your minds on things above,
not on earthly things.
—Colossians 3:2

*W*ho wouldn't want to get married? Who wouldn't want a companion for life to share their joys and trials? Who wouldn't want someone to care for them when they were sick? Who wouldn't want someone to encourage them when they were down? Who wouldn't want someone who knew them completely and still loved them? Who wouldn't want someone who loved them just as they were, yet loved them enough to encourage them to become all that they could be? Who wouldn't want someone to tell them that they had done a great job today, that they were beautiful, talented, and fun to live with? Who wouldn't want someone they could run around the house with naked and have sex with whenever and wherever they pleased without any shame? Who wouldn't want that?!

God's plan is designed to give us all this and more. His plan is perfect and cannot be improved on. And yet for many, such intimacy is elusive and their marriage is failing miserably in delivering what they were hoping for.

I smile whenever I remember the time I asked a good friend returning from his honeymoon how it was. "That sex thing is harder than they make it out to be." No one thinks you need to learn to have good sex, and few think you are going to need to work at having a good marriage.

One of my privileges as a pastor is performing wedding ceremonies. As we meet together to plan their ceremony, I don't ask the couple, "Now, how long do you plan to be married? If you just want a 2-year marriage, then we'll have a quick 10-minute ceremony. If you plan to stay married for 10 years, the ceremony is a bit more complicated. If you plan on a marriage lasting 30 years or more, then the details of the ceremony are numerous." Of course not! Because every couple that comes down the aisle expects to be happily married forever and ever. That's what Disney and *Bride* magazine say. Unfortunately, according to statistics, that is not happening in the vast majority of marriages.

We are facing a crisis in the U.S. today. About 50% of recent marriages are projected to end in divorce,[2] and the majority of those staying married are not experiencing the delight they had hoped for in matrimony. Many couples that seem to have it all together on the outside are actually struggling to realize all they had dreamed their marriage would be.

If airlines crashed 50% of the time, would we fly? If throttles stuck in our cars 50% of the time, would we drive? If you got sick 50% of the time you ate chicken, would you eat chicken? If your computer crashed 50% of the time, would you buy the same brand of computer?

This year alone over 2 million couples will say, "I do." Unfortunately, over 1 million will say, "I wish I hadn't," and will end their marriage in divorce.[3] We have seen an alarming increase in the number of couples coming to see us for counseling that are ready to call it quits, many of whom have been married for two years or less!

But here is the kicker: people are continuing to get married!

We recently met with a wealthy professional couple who were really struggling in their marriage. As they told us about her not feeing secure in the relationship and his feeling controlled by her, she said, "I have never felt secure since I was forced to sign the pre-nuptial agreement." "Then why did you sign it?" we asked. "He said he wouldn't marry me if I didn't sign it." At this point he interrupted and said, "I haven't worked this hard, for this long, to lose half of my assets to her if we divorce." It's no surprise that intimacy was eluding this couple.

Something at the core of human beings longs to be married ...

So why did this couple get married? Why wouldn't they both get everything they wanted simply by living together? What difference does a piece of paper make?

Something at the core of human beings longs to be married and to have lifelong security and exclusive intimacy with another individual. We are not designed to be alone.

Consider Adam in the Garden of Eden, who had a perfect relationship with God, the animals, and nature. Nevertheless, regarding this apparent state of perfection, God—for the first time—says something is not good. For six days, He had continued to say that everything was good. Sin had not entered the Garden yet—so what could be wrong? What was wrong was that there was no one with whom Adam could be intimate (in every sense of the word). In addition to designing us for relationship with the Trinity, God designed us to need an intimate relationship with other human beings. For most humans, this need is met in its fullest form in marriage.

And so the question we face is, if marriage is all God's idea, why is it so difficult for so many?

LONGING FOR INTIMACY

The LORD God said, "It is not good for the man to be alone. I will make a helper suitable for him." —Genesis 2:18

We were created to be in community. God made us to want to share life with another. God gave Eve to Adam as a "suitable helper," and together they were to care for the Garden, have communion with God, and enjoy each other's nakedness. We yearn for what we were created to experience: intimacy with another human being.

Virginia was meeting with a woman who was in an abusive relationship with a man. She shared how badly he treated her emotionally, physically, and sexually. When Virginia asked why she didn't leave him, she explained, "I just don't want to be alone."

We were created for and long for relationship. Often, in an attempt to avoid being alone, couples cohabit and miss out on the fullness of God's design.

THE DILEMMA OF SELFISHNESS

It is perplexing to consider why Adam and Eve, after living in the Garden of Eden and enjoying an ongoing relationship of intimacy with each other and with God, would allow something as "small" as a piece of fruit to destroy the idyllic life they were living. Because of Adam and Eve's sinful, selfish choice, instead of enjoying paradise in close fellowship with their Creator, they were now scurrying to find leaves to sew together because their sin made them ashamed of their nakedness. Having sinned against God, they now played hide and seek with Him. How odd is it that Adam and Eve would throw away an eternity of sinless relationship with God for a moment of pleasure? Perhaps it's not quite so surprising as we might think. Consider how frequently we each make selfish choices that take us away from what could have been if only we had honored God's design. I can think of many occasions on which I was enjoying an idyllic time with Virginia, but then selfishly did something that destroyed the moment and robbed us of what might have been.

We recently met with a couple that, up until the previous year, seemed to "have it all." They were both physically beautiful. Many called them the "Barbie and Ken couple" in their community. He had a great job as a vice principal at the local high school. They were lay leaders of the youth group at church and were seen as the "perfect" Christian family in town.

When we met with them, he was living with his parents, coaching kickball and teaching 4th grade. They were no longer leading the youth group; many in their church and community shunned them. Instead of being admired as the kids that had the cool dad at school, their two teenagers walked the halls aware that many were snickering at them. What was it that could have turned this family's dream life into a nightmare? Nothing much, merely a sexual indiscretion with the high school secretary. He had it all, and he threw it away for a few nights of "passion."

This story reminds me of King David after he committed adultery with Bathsheba and murdered her husband. Through the prophet Nathan, God spoke to David, saying:

> *"This is what the Lord, the God of Israel, says: 'I anointed you king over Israel, and I delivered you from the hand of Saul. I gave your master's house to you, and your master's wives into your arms. I gave you the house of Israel and Judah. And if all this had been too little, I would have given you even more. Why did you despise the word of the Lord by doing what is evil in his eyes?'"*
> —*2 Samuel 12:7b–9a*

Satan is always eager to dangle what God has forbidden so that he can destroy what God has designed for our blessing. God is saying to us, in essence: "I have given you so much—and if this is too little, I would have given you much more. Why have you despised my word and done what is evil in My sight?"

In his wonderful book *Sacred Marriage*, author Gary Thomas describes the relationship of marriage and selfishness:

> Marriage creates a situation in which our desire to be served and coddled can be replaced with a more noble desire to serve others—even to sacrifice for others. This is a call for both husbands and wives. The beauty of marriage is that it confronts our selfishness and demands our service twenty-four hours a day. When we're most tired, most worn down, and feeling more sorry for ourselves than we ever have before, we have the opportunity to confront feelings of self-pity by getting up and serving our mate.
>
> The reason this thought may not have been obvious to so many for so long is that the vast majority of people do not enter marriage with a view to becoming a servant. The marriage relationship is often seen as a selfish one because our motivations for marrying often are selfish. But my desire is to reclaim marriage as one of the most selfless states a Christian can enter.
>
> To fully sanctify the marital relationship, we must live it together as Jesus lived His life—embracing the discipline of sacrifice and service as a daily practice. In the same way that Jesus gave His body for us, we are to lay down our energy, our bodies, and our lives for others.[4]

Listening to Satan's disguised voice saying "I can give you more" often robs us of what God desires for us to experience. It is not good to be alone, and yet we act independently and selfishly, so often missing out on what could have been.

SEEKING A MODEL FOR INTIMACY

Seeking happiness in marriage can be like seeking the perfect weight-loss program. We continue to try program after program, only to learn that without self-discipline and a commitment to changing our lifestyle, all of them will eventually fail. In like manner, many couples are seeking what they hoped for through the reading of self-help books and/or experimenting with various marriage models in hopes of finding one that "works." Some of these marriage models are:

+ **The "50/50" model:** Many couples enter marriage determined to make the relationship "equal." Back when we were living in seminary housing, we heard a young couple yelling at each other as they walked down the hall.

  "No, it's your night to cook, I did it yesterday."

  "Yeah, but I did your dishes last night."

  "That's because I was editing your paper."

  "You didn't even cook last night, we ate leftovers."

  Any time we start keeping score, we both lose.

+ **The "No Rules, Just Love" model:** In this model the work is not assigned; it is motivated by love. Each spouse should just do what he or she wants to do, when he or she wants to do it, because no one should have to do what they don't want to do—love is doing what comes naturally. Unfortunately, sacrificially putting one's spouse ahead of one's own desires seldom comes naturally.

+ **The "Male/Female Role" model:** This model offers clearly laid out lines of responsibility that follow traditional gender roles. This is simply how it should be! The most general model says men should care for outside the house, women for the inside. (This is especially appealing to men when the couple lives in a condo, with outside maintenance and yard service included in the association fees.) More specific applications have men paying all the bills, women doing all the cooking, men fixing anything that breaks, women changing all the diapers, etc. Unfortunately, in this model the male or female may not have all the gifts or abilities needed to carry out their "roles."

• **The "Family of Origin" model:** In this model, husband and wife each know "how it should be done," because it was modeled for them in their families of origin. Our daughter and son-in-law experienced this upon unloading their first groceries as a couple. As Kari went to put the potatoes under the sink, Gabe asked, "Why are you putting the potatoes under the sink?"

"That's where they go," Kari replied.

"Who puts potatoes under the sink??" Gabe asked, a note of sarcasm in his voice.

In a strong voice and with equal conviction, Kari said, "My mother does!" Often we don't know exactly why our parents did what they did, but if it was good enough for them, it will be good enough for us—as long as both the husband's and the wife's families did life the same way! The obvious flaw in this model is that families of origin can indeed be quite different.

• **The "Meet My Needs" model:** This model is a bit of a newcomer on the scene now that we have so many self-help books that tell us what our needs are. This model in essence says, "I have needs, and if my spouse does not meet them, then my acting out is my spouse's fault and that is why I am not the spouse I should be." The problem with this model is that it tries to make your spouse responsible for your sinful actions if she or he doesn't meet your "needs."

• **The "Parallel Lives" model:** Those who are a bit older and established when they are married often choose this model. They are glad to get married, but they do not plan on drastically changing their work, friends, or lifestyle. In essence the understanding is, "You do your thing and I'll do my thing—and when we are together, it will be a wonderful addition to our lives." These couples often live together in peace, yet seldom experience marital oneness and intimacy.

Not every marriage that uses one of these models is headed for divorce court, but the couples who adopt them are far from experiencing what they had hoped for in marriage. The common thread in the above is "marriage is about me, meeting my needs, mirroring my past experience, and making me happy." It might be that you had expected that he would always be interested in how your day went, or that she would always think you were terrific, or that he would prefer to spend the day with you over golfing with the guys, or that she would still put you first even after having children, or that he would be glad to cuddle at night, or that she couldn't keep her hands off of you.

EXPECTATIONS FOR MARRIAGE

Many of us come into marriage with unrealistic expectations.

About a month before our own wedding, Virginia and I were talking about how much we were looking forward to having sex for the first time and with each other. I remember Virginia saying, "I don't know how we'll ever get any work done after we are married—we'll just be making love all day." Well, guess what? We've gotten a lot of work done! Some expectations are delusional.

Someone once said that our level of satisfaction in marriage is the difference between what we expected in marriage and what we experience in marriage. Many of us enter marriage today with totally unrealistic expectations. These may come from our families of origin, or from movies, music, fantasies, hopes, or dreams. Wherever these unrealistic expectations come from, they often lead to great disappointment and dissatisfaction. It is our responsibility to have a realistic grasp on marriage so that we can appropriately respond to different circumstances in a way that

47

honors God and serves our spouse. Let's examine a few unrealistic expectations, balanced with a more accurate picture of what real marriages are like.

Unrealistic expectations	Realistic expectations
Marriage will be easy.	Marriage is hard work.
We will always agree.	We will sharpen each other through discussion.
He will never notice other women.	He will remain faithful in heart and body to me.
She will always be my cheerleader.	Her DNA from the fall will be to control me.
He will always want to talk.	We will need to learn to communicate despite our uniqueness as male and female.
We will have sex all the time.	We are to express love in a mutually satisfying way.
We will always like the same things.	We will seek to know and meet our spouse's desires.

EXPECTATIONS AND INTIMACY

About ten years ago we took a group of families to the country of Trinidad and Tobago for a family mission trip. Never having been to the area before, I was expecting that my last shower for the week would be the shower I took the morning we headed for the airport. When we arrived in Trinidad and were shown our accommodations, I was pleasantly surprised to see we did in fact have a "shower." The shower "head" was the cut-off end of a ¾-inch PVC pipe. The temperature of the shower was whatever was provided by nature—at best, lukewarm. I was elated! Here my expectations were "no showers," but I had lukewarm water coming out of a ¾-inch PVC pipe.

About two weeks later, the two of us were speaking at a marriage conference held in a five-star resort. The suite we were given was about half the size of our home, including two bedrooms, living room, and kitchen. The bathroom was enormous and boasted a gorgeous Jacuzzi tub and a huge shower with four pulsing shower heads. I awakened the first morning and got up to take a long hot shower, only to discover that the water temperature matched that of the water in Trinidad: lukewarm. I stormed out of shower and called the front desk. My comments were not kind, because my expectations were not realized. The point

> *Many couples today have simply never seen what a marriage of sacrificial love looks like.*

is obvious: same water temperature, different response, all based on expectations.

So is the problem in marriage today simply that we are expecting too much? Would it be better to expect cold-water showers and be happy if we get lukewarm?

The description of marriage given in scripture is anything but lukewarm. Scripture commands husbands to love their wives as Christ loved the church—and His love was certainly not lukewarm. Christ's love for the church was sacrificial. He always put the needs of the church ahead of His own. Even when He got away by Himself, it was to be renewed in order to better serve. Wives are told to respect and submit to their husbands "as unto the Lord." Another way to look at it is that wives are called to submit to their husbands in the same way Christ submitted to the Father—which is anything but mediocre.

Many couples today have simply never seen what a marriage of sacrificial love looks like. Just this week a woman came up to us after we spoke at a church and said she had just told her boyfriend the night before that she was never going to marry because she had never seen a good marriage.

For many years we have been program directors for a family camp that "employs" about 40 college-aged students each summer. Garth and Rosemary were in their 60s when we first asked them to be on our staff, and they continued to serve with us for the next 15 summers. Over the years, many people asked us what the role of this older couple was. "Just to hang around our staff," we replied. "They are older, love each other, love the Lord, love

> *Strong marriages are not built on "personal satisfaction" as much as on knowledge, decisions, and sacrifice.*

serving—and they exude joy. We want our staff to see how great it is to grow older and be madly in love with your spouse, with the Lord, and with life." We kept telling our young staff that Garth and Rosemary did not just decide to like each other when they were 65—they made intentional decisions over the entire course of their marriage to love and serve the Lord and each other. Their marriage is anything but mediocre.

The story is told of a young man—back before 9/11, when greeting deplaning passengers at the gate was still allowed—who, while waiting at the gate to board his flight, was watching passengers as they disembarked. He couldn't help but notice a returning husband passionately embrace his wife as his children leapt around with excitement. The young man approached this family and said to the husband, "Excuse me, but how long have you been gone?" thinking the answer would be a month or more.

"One day," replied the husband.

"Wow, when I am married I hope I have a marriage like yours!"

"You don't 'hope', son. You decide."

Neither this couple nor Garth and Rosemary merely "hoped" for a good marriage; they chose to have one. They didn't experience a marriage without trials, disappointments, or unmet expectations, but they definitely were intentional in honoring and serving each other.

Strong marriages are not built on "personal satisfaction" as much as on knowledge, decisions, and sacrifice. Our culture tells us to seek our own happiness, take care of #1, realize your potential, pamper yourself; "you deserve a break today," "have it your way," and so on. In the words of Dr. Phil, how's that workin' out?

A jewelry store near San Luis Obispo, California, advertised on a billboard along Highway 101 during the month before Valentine's Day: "Your relationship may not last, but our diamonds will."

While it may be true that diamonds last forever, they will never satisfy our souls. Let's continue to explore "God's billboard" for relationships that will last a lifetime and satisfy our souls. We were designed for intimacy, but what the world is prescribing seldom brings the intimacy we long for. Since God designed us and also designed marriage, let's start in the Garden and see where we went wrong and what we can do to "get back to Eden."

When we put our spouse's needs above our own,
not only will they feel loved,
but it will propel our marriage towards greater intimacy.

Reminders

☑ We were "hard wired" to desire community.

☑ It is not good for Adam, or for us, to be alone.

☑ With divorce rampant, clearly most are not experiencing the expected intimacy in marriage.

☑ Selfishness is often at the root of marital discord.

☑ Many "types" of marriages strive to deliver, but most seem focused on self-satisfaction.

☑ Much of our dissatisfaction with marriage comes from unrealistic expectations.

☑ The answer to unrealistic expectations, however, is not to expect mediocre marriages.

☑ The example for marriage of the relationship between Christ and the Church is anything but mediocre.

☑ We often lack examples of vital marriages.

☑ Vital marriages are built on intentionality and decisions of the will, not simply on hope.

For Couples

Questions

1. In what ways has marriage exceeded your expectations?

2. In what areas have your expectations not been realized?

3. What do you think "intimacy" in marriage should look like?

APPlication

• Do one thing each day to let your spouse know you love and appreciate them. It could be a note, flowers, gift, or a specific act of kindness they would appreciate.

• Each day this week, share with your spouse about something you are facing that day. Each of you pray for the other before you leave home in the morning. (This does not need to take more than 5 minutes. Husbands, initiate the prayer on the odd-numbered days, wives on the even-numbered days.)

For Groups

1. Share what you think are the most unrealistic expectations most couples come into marriage with.

2. Why do you think cohabitation has never been more common than it is now?

3. In spite of this, why do you think couples are still flocking to get married?

4. What are the most common ways you see selfishness expressed in marriages today?

5. Which of the six models of marriage do you see most in action today?

6. Read Genesis 2:15–25.

   • What would you say are God's expectations for marriage according to this passage?

   • How does God's list contrast with what most couples expect from marriage?

7. What practical steps can you take this week to more fully experience God's design for intimacy?

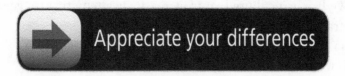

Appreciate your differences

I praise you because I am fearfully and wonderfully made;
your works are wonderful, I know that full well.
—Psalm 139:14

Virginia and I were married on April 24, 1976. We spent our first night at the beautiful, historic, 4-star, beachfront Hotel Del Coronado in San Diego, California, spending $60 for the night—but hey, you only have one honeymoon night. We spent our second night at Motel 6 in Goleta, California, near Santa Barbara, spending $6. Yes, that's why it was called Motel 6. We had been married less than 48 hours and marriage was great, life was great, sex was great, and this marriage thing was a piece of cake. We were obviously perfect for each other. We were driving on the very picturesque and romantic Highway 1 along the Pacific Coast near Big Sur when a squirrel darted out in front of our car. At the exact same moment, Virginia and I glanced back; Virginia cried out, "Ohhh . . . " and I yelled, "Got it!"

We both laugh now, but she was not laughing then. Her thought at the time was "What is *wrong* with this man? I married a man who shouts 'Got it!' when he kills a defenseless squirrel?"

Now, I am not one who maims or kills animals intentionally, but that day we realized that while we might be perfect for each other, we were certainly not the same.

We live in a culture that is increasingly attempting to "gender neutralize" us. We are told in so many ways that men and women really are not different, that boys and girls are the same except for physiology and it's our environment that shapes them. In marriages and in the church, we work hard to prove that there really are not any roles or responsibilities designed primarily for men or women.

Our marriages were designed to reflect the Godhead.

It is our goal in this chapter to use God's word to help us understand how He has intentionally designed men and women differently. Though these differences can often be a cause of great conflict, they were actually designed to bring us closer together.

IF ALL ELSE FAILS, READ THE MANUAL

A few weeks ago, I borrowed my friends' Lexus Hybrid SUV. Upon returning it, I told them that I had filled it up with regular unleaded gas. They graciously thanked me. Last week, I borrowed their car again. They very kindly said I could use their credit card to fill it with gas when I was done and that they always use premium gasoline. They put premium in because the manufacturer recommends it for the best performance and longest life of the car. After that exchange, I thought about how putting regular gas in the tank regularly might cause the car to not perform as well. Naively, I might then conclude something was wrong with the Lexus. But, no, the problem would not have been the car, but that I had not read the operator's manual to see how to best care for the car.

I have another friend who bought a sports car and loved it. After only 35,000 miles, its engine froze. Upon examination, it was discovered that he had never had its oil changed!

Unless you maintain cars properly, you will be disappointed in their performance. Similarly, many of us put only "regular gas" into our marriages and neglect to "change the oil," and then are dumbfounded when the marriage functions poorly or seems to stop working at all. Nothing is wrong with marriage, but many of us have not heeded the "manufacturer's guidelines."

God's design for marriage is included in His "Operator's Manual"—the Bible. When we fail to understand the manual, our marriages may still work, but not at the level the Designer has intended the operators to experience.

MARRIAGE AS A REFLECTION OF THE GODHEAD

Our marriages were designed to reflect the Godhead. We are created in the very image of God! In the Godhead we find incredible intimacy, unity, and oneness. We also find diversity: consider how very different each member of the Trinity is. They each have different roles, yet no one member of the Trinity is less valuable than the other members. Therefore it should not surprise us, as image bearers of the Godhead, that we have uniqueness as individuals yet are called to live together in complete unity. Genesis tells us that God made male and female in His image. We are married to another image bearer of the King of King and Lord of Lords, the Creator of the universe, the One who sustains every creature that lives on the planet. We are married to someone created in the very image of God.

Perfect unity and intimacy are seen in the Trinity, and yet the three are each different and distinct: God the Father, God the Son, and God the Holy Spirit. The irony seen in their relationship is that as they each live out their distinctiveness, their intimacy and unity are realized fully.

The Bible teaches us that we don't have to give up our uniqueness as male and female to experience intimacy. In fact, intimacy will be most fully experienced within a marriage only when husband and wife are learning to grow distinctly as godly man and godly woman.

GOD'S DESIGN FOR PARTNERSHIP

The LORD God said, "It is not good for the man to be alone. I will make a helper suitable for him."

Now the LORD God had formed out of the ground all the beasts of the field and all the birds of the air. He brought them to the man to see what he would name them; and whatever the man called each living creature, that was its name. So the man gave names to all the livestock, the birds of the air and all the beasts of the field.

But for Adam no suitable helper was found. So the LORD God caused the man to fall into a deep sleep; and while he was sleeping, he took one of the man's ribs and closed up the place with flesh. Then the LORD God made a woman from the rib he had taken out of the man, and he brought her to the man.

The man said,
"This is now bone of my bones
and flesh of my flesh;
she shall be called 'woman,'
for she was taken out of man."

For this reason a man will leave his father and mother and be united to his wife, and they will become one flesh.

The man and his wife were both naked, and they felt no shame. —Genesis 2:18–25

Imagine Adam's delight: in addition to living in a perfect paradise, just when he thought it couldn't get any better, God brought him a little helper woman to clean up after him, cook for him, and pick up his clothes (oh, wait—that wasn't necessary, he was naked!). No, this is *not* what God was saying. What He was saying was, "Adam! You need *help*! I am going to give you a partner to come alongside you, one who can talk with you, support you, encourage you, and be a helper to you."

Often, when we hear the word "help," we think of someone who is "less" than us. When our own children were young, they were occasionally hired by mothers to be "mother's helpers"—that is, they could help with the children, but were not old enough to be left alone to care for the children. They were "less than" a real babysitter.

When we are being honest, we will acknowledge that there are many places in the world and many times when women have been regarded as "less" than men. Virginia and I were recently in Uganda and were teaching there on God's design for marriage. In Africa, it is still customary for a man to pay the father of the bride anywhere from 4 to 8 cows before taking the daughter as his wife. One woman confided in us that when she is not pleasing to her husband, he reminds her that he paid 6 cows for her and therefore she must do as he says. She said, "I feel as if he 'bought' me, and sees me as his property instead of as his wife, his partner, his equal."

The Hebrew phrase translated as "a helper suitable" includes two words: *ēzer k'negdô*. The first word, translated "helper", implies someone who assists and encourages. "Help" provides support for what is lacking in the one who needs help. "Helper suitable for him" means "a helper matching his distinctiveness". It certainly points to one who is fit to stand before the man, opposite him, as his counterpart, companion, and complement. There is no sense of inferiority, subordination, or servitude implied here. Rather, it is one who is "like him" but "like opposite him" (to give a literal rendering).

This same word *ēzer* "helper" is most often used in the Old Testament to refer to God. Twice it is used to refer to Eve, three times it is used to refer to nations that provided military assistance to Israel, but the other 16 times it is used in reference to God as a helper. All 21 uses are talking about a vital, powerful, and rescuing kind of help.

So, far from woman being created as a "little helper" for Adam, she was created to come alongside him and help him be more fully who God designed him to be.

DESIGNED FOR DIGNITY

It was an early evening in April of 2005. I was coming out of a store in downtown Boston when I observed a couple about 100 feet from me, arguing with each other. The arm gestures indicated that this was more than a small tiff. It was a full-blown, fully charged fight. And then it happened: he spit in her face. She immediately got behind him and followed him with her head down until they reached their car; they got in, and they drove off.

How despicable. I couldn't imagine how a man could spit in the face of another human being, someone created in the very image of God! It was then, as I considered this, that a voice rang in my head. It was as if God were standing there talking to me. "You shouldn't have such a hard time with this, since you have spit in Virginia's face. I know you haven't used saliva, but you have said unkind words to her. You have insulted her. You have intentionally used your tongue to hurt her. How could you do this to someone created in my image? Shouldn't the fact that she has been created in my image cause you to treat her with kindness and dignity?"

If you were to shut this book now, grasp this truth, and apply it, we believe the cost of the book would be worth it, even if you paid full price.

It is interesting how often it seems to be easier to treat those outside our family with more dignity than those inside. I love the cartoon of a pastor heading out the door to work, while his wife shouts after him, "Why don't you do it opposite this week? Be nice at home, and a jerk at church!" It may get a chuckle here, but it's too often not a joke in our own homes.

It is not uncommon for us to meet with a couple where one or both parties use as their defense, "No one else complains that I have a temper" (or "... am a nag," "... am indifferent," "... am controlling," etc.). This defense is, in actuality, an indictment against them. What would happen if you treated your wife the same way you do the women at work? What would happen if you treated your husband the same way you treat your children's teacher at school? For some reason, many of us let go of patience and courtesy at home, thinking our mates will understand or at least put up with it.

Jesus takes this to the next level when He differentiates between those who truly do and do not know Him:

> *"'For I was hungry and you gave me something to eat, I was thirsty and you gave me something to drink, I was a stranger and you invited me in, I needed clothes and you clothed me, I was sick and you looked after me, I was in prison and you came to visit me.'*
>
> *"Then the righteous will answer him, 'Lord, when did we see you hungry and feed you, or thirsty and give you something to drink? When did we see you a stranger and invite you in, or needing clothes and clothe you? When did we see you sick or in prison and go to visit you?'*
>
> *"The King will reply, 'I tell you the truth, whatever you did for one of the least of these brothers of mine, you did for me.'"*
>
> *—Matthew 25:35–40*

Certainly "the least of these" includes our spouse. Most of us would treat our spouse with kindness, patience, and consideration if our pastor were in the house. Well, Jesus is in the house—and He is taking note of how we are treating those made in His image.

My "marriage paraphrase" of the Matthew 25 passage above is this: " 'Remember the time I just needed to talk and you put down the remote and listened to me? And I remember the time I forgot your birthday and you didn't make me feel like a loser. I also remember you taking the kids out for the morning so I could sleep in and then take a long bath. I remember the time you sent the kids away and planned a romantic night just for the two of us.' Then you will say, 'Lord, when did this happen?' He will say, 'Remember the kindnesses you show to your spouse? You are not really doing it for your spouse only; you are also doing it for me.' "

Yes, Jesus *is* in the house, and how we treat each other brings Him either sadness or delight.

Dan Allender puts it very well in his book, *Intimate Allies*:

> Do we see our spouses as reflecting the face of God? Or are we captured more by their imperfections and our own disappointment? To view our spouses from the lens of glory is to be overwhelmed by the privilege of being face-to-face with a creature who mirrors God. Consequently, as partners, we will feel more overwhelmed with gratitude than disappointment; we will experience more joy than bitterness. Glory requires a submission to mystery; it demands our heart, soul, mind, and energy.[5]

GOD'S DESIGN FOR DIVERSITY

> *So God created man in his own image,*
> *in the image of God he created him;*
> *male and female he created them.* —Genesis 1:27

Being created in the image of God not only gives us dignity, but also speaks to our diversity. The Trinity are equal but diverse; they are not the same. Father, Son, and Holy Spirit are equal but have unique functions. In like manner, while we are equal as male and female, we are not the same.

In the scripture above, we see the dignity of both man and woman, each made in the image of God, but also the distinctiveness of both man and woman.

God *intentionally* made us to be opposite each other, by design. This should help to depersonalize some of the ways one's spouse's "oppositeness" may be an irritant; God made him or her that way on purpose. (We're not talking here about sinfulness, but uniqueness.)

> *Being created in the image of God not only gives us dignity, but also speaks to our diversity.*

What an amazing privilege it is for us, as finite beings, to reflect the infinite, perfect beauty of God. And we are able to do so only in the complexity and distinctiveness of both sexes. Both men and women are made in the image of God. Both are necessary in order to fully reflect God; one alone is not only incomplete but also inadequate to reflect His glory. Men and women reflect different aspects of God's nature.

> This foundational teaching about gender emphasizes an important truth right from the beginning. Men and women, though different, are equal in the eyes of God. Neither is closer to God; they are both his image.[6]

As we look at some of the "intentional differences" in our design by God, remember that His design of "like but opposite" was done before sin entered the world.

In fact, even the way our brains function is unique to male and female. Barbara and Dennis Rainey write about this:

> Simply put, a man's brain operates specifically, while a woman's operates holistically. The right hemisphere of a man's brain can and does operate without the left being involved, and vice versa. A woman's brain uses and integrates both hemispheres simultaneously. Thus, a man can give more focused attention to his work or project, while his wife can be tuned in to everything around her. This makes her more perceptive of people and their feelings than her husband is, and it enables her, especially if she is a mother, to know what is going on in every part of the house at once.
>
> I now understand why Dennis can be reading the paper and not know that the children, a few feet away, are terrorizing one another. Rather than get angry with him for his apparent non-involvement, I realize that one side of his brain is "off" and that he's just being himself, a man.
>
> Also, when he comes home from work, the children sometimes scream for his attention, yet he doesn't seem to hear them. I tell them, "Relax, kids, your daddy's not home yet!"
>
> Exasperated, they reply, "Yes he is, Mom. He's standing right here."
>
> But I tell them, "We know he's home, but he doesn't know it yet!"[7]

One way to express appreciation for your spouse's uniqueness is to ask for your spouse's opinion. Another way is when your spouse acts or sees something differently than you, to say, "Wow, that's interesting; I never would have thought of it that way" rather than "How do you come up with this stuff? What's wrong with you?"

DIFFERENT IS GOOD

Many aspects of our uniqueness that we find interesting before marriage can become irritating after marriage. We will now look at three specific areas—communication, sexuality, and temperaments—which often cause marital conflict, but point to the unique ways in which God has designed us differently.

Communication

It is said that men generally have fewer words than women, that women tend to want to process while men want to fix, and that women are into building relationships while men are focused on tasks. Certainly this is not true across the board, but it is true in many homes. It is worth investigating how God has wired us differently.

When a man comes home and is asked how his day was and he grunts "fine," it is an affront to his wife, who wants to process the day. When I come home after a long day, Virginia will often ask, "How was your day?"

"Fine," I answer.

"What do you mean, 'fine'?", she asks.

"My day was fine, is what I meant."

"Just fine?"

"Yeah, just fine."

She then launches into what seems to be an unending litany of questions. "Well, what did you do today? Did you meet anyone new? Did you go out for lunch? Where did you go? Who went with you? What did you eat? You didn't order dessert, did you? Did everyone pay individually or did you split the tab? Did you walk to the restaurant or drive? Were you late back to work? Do you think people not invited to lunch feel left out? Do you think they can't afford lunch out, or would just prefer eating at the office?"

A few years ago, a friend of mine called to ask me if we could have lunch the next day. The conversation went something like this: "Paul, I was wondering if we could catch lunch together tomorrow?"

"Sounds good, how about noon at the Sheraton?" I replied.

"Great, see you there," was his response, and he hung up.

Soon after that, the phone rang for Virginia. She was on the phone for 45 minutes, talking. I was in and out of the room during her long conversation, so when she hung up I asked her what the call had been about.

"Oh, nothing," she said, "we were just setting up lunch for tomorrow."

"What are you going to talk about?" I asked. "You just talked for 45 minutes!"

Women tend to be more relational when they talk, while men tend to be more task-focused. Recently, Virginia was getting ice from a coffee shop for her Patriots travel mug, which she carries with her wherever we go. She asked the employee for ice, explaining that we are from Boston but when she's on the West Coast, she loves to come into this shop because its franchise has such great ice—and they were off and running in a lengthy conversation. But if I wanted ice, I would go into the coffee shop and say, "Could I have some ice, please? Thank you," and that would be it.

Men's tendency is to think, "I'd be happier if she talked less." Women ask, "Why can't he talk more?" We have found it helpful to remember that it was God's idea to create us in His image and not each other's. Instead of resenting our differences, we have tried to come to the place of appreciating our differences. The reason we have friends is because I am married to my relational spouse Virginia. But when we are in a hurry and we need "ice" and nothing more, Virginia sends me in, alone.

If instead of focusing on our spouses' areas of "annoyance" we focus on how God has "fearfully and wonderfully" made them different from us and affirm them for this, we will experience more of the partnership and intimacy God intended for us.

Sexuality

Another area in which we have been uniquely designed as male and female is in our views of sexuality.

We have some dear friends who tell the story of one morning in their house after all their children had left for school. After the husband showered and dried himself off, he proceeded to flop on his back on the bed buck-naked. His wife came into the room and continued to talk about the day—Jill had ballet at 3:30, Jeff had soccer at 4:00. She went on to say perhaps they could grab a quick dinner out since they both should be at the PTA meeting at school that evening at 7:00. Then she started to walk out the door, at which point he said from his naked perch, "Don't you notice anything?" "Yes," she said as she left the room, "you better get some clothes on or you'll be late for work!" But if his wife had been the one lying naked on the bed, he would likely have cancelled his day and joined her! We think *so* differently about the area of sexuality.

Another husband and wife had a horrible day. They bickered and fought and snapped at each other all day long. Finally, at 11 pm, after getting the kids put to bed and finishing up some chores, they fell into bed, exhausted.

"Want to do it?" the husband asked.

"Do what?" the wife responded, sarcastically.

"Have sex," replied the husband.

"I don't even *like* you," she snapped.

"So?" was his response—and he meant it.

Another friend arrived home late one night after being gone for two days. He slipped into bed quietly and noticed his wife moving. "Are you awake?" he asked softly. "Yes," she said. He then started to make a sexual advance, to which she responded, "Not *that* awake."

We have been created by God to look at our sexuality differently. A man is visually stimulated, aroused quickly, and thinks about sex frequently. Often a nice Christian wife looks at her husband

and thinks, "Pervert!" Perhaps, but not necessarily so—just male. Women were not designed the same way. A wife gets undressed in front of her husband, he's aroused. The husband gets undressed in front of his wife, she's tired—or just wants a hug. We are not designed the same, and it was God's idea to do this. However, this never gives a husband an excuse to sin by saying "God made me this way."

Knowing that God is for sex and has our good in mind, it should depersonalize our frustration with each other when we realize how differently we approach this area of our lives.

This may be helpful to know intellectually, but it still leaves us with this question: If God wanted our sexual life to be one of intimacy, oneness, unity, and joy, why did He give us such different approaches to sexual expression?

Instead of experiencing frustration with our differences, our confidence in God's good design should cause us to explore how we can serve each other sacrificially, even in the area of our sexuality. Putting your spouse ahead of yourself in this area can increase your intimacy rather than detract from it.

Temperaments

Another area, not gender related, has to do with how God intentionally created people with a diverse range of temperaments. Personality differences we find so attractive and endearing before marriage have the potential to become irritants after marriage.

A system that we have found helpful for understanding differences in temperament is the Myers-Briggs Type Indicator.[8] It is a temperament assessment tool that helps us to identify our primary operating system: the way we "do" life, if you will. For instance, I am an introvert. That does not mean that I do not do well in groups or in front of an audience, but it does mean that I need solitude to recharge my batteries. Virginia, on the other hand, is an extravert and is recharged by being with people.

In 2003 I decided to drive a car from Boston, Massachusetts, to Stockton, California, by myself, to surprise our middle daughter Lisa with a much-needed automobile. When we tell that story you can distinguish an introvert from an extravert from their reaction. The introvert says, "Cool, I wish I could do that!" whereas the extravert asks, "Couldn't you find anyone willing to go with you?"

Another example: Virginia is a person of order. She believes that everything has a home and should stay in that home unless it is being used, and then it should be

> *We have all been created in the image of God.*

returned to that home—things like staplers, keys, phones, and remote controls. Well, she ended up marrying someone who believes everything is homeless. I leave things in the last place I used them. In my defense, I am what is referred to in Myers-Briggs language as an intuitive, which means I am wired to be creative, a bit of a dreamer, and never quite where I appear to be. Virginia, on the other hand, is very present. Again, these differences have the ability to cause significant conflict. Virginia could easily ask me, "Why don't you become more organized and responsible?" I, on the other hand, could ask, "Why don't you ever create anything? Why are you so predictable?" But it is through sacrificially loving our spouse and seeking to understand their different wiring that we are able to experience the partnership and intimacy that being married to someone "fearfully and wonderfully made" can bring.

We have all been created in the image of God. That gives us both dignity and diversity. We know that God declares that in marriage we become one, and He desires for us to experience unity and oneness. We also know that it was God's intention to make us unique as individuals and distinctively male and female. We experience this in how we approach our communication, sexuality, and temperaments. We also know that He desires that we honor each other with our uniqueness. We know that at the end of day six of creation God didn't say, "Okay, but this needs some work." He said *"very good!"*

> *Then God said, "Let us make man in our image, in our likeness, and let them rule over the fish of the sea and the birds of the air, over the livestock, over all the earth, and over all the creatures that move along the ground."* ... *God saw all that he had made, and it was very good. And there was evening, and there was morning—the sixth day.* —Genesis 1:26, 31

BETTER TOGETHER

God says it is very good that we are different. So if it is very good, why is it so very hard? At the deepest level, perhaps, it is a misunderstanding of the Trinity. The Godhead is fully expressed through the *cooperation* of the Father, Son, and Holy Spirit, not because they are the *same*. They have unique functions, but operate as one. They have different responsibilities, but are equal. They have distinct roles, but are not in a power struggle to prove who is best.

Virginia and I speak at a weekly Bible study with couples from the New England Patriots, and therefore it is a ministry requirement that I listen to sports radio and follow football quite closely. It is always interesting during free agency or the draft to hear the commentators discuss strategy. I never hear a comment like, "The Patriots have the best punter in the league, so they will be going after two more punters in the draft." What you do hear is, "When Teddy Bruschi left the Patriots, they went looking for a new leader to fill the void left at linebacker." Diversity in talent and skill makes for a better sports team—and a better office group or pastoral staff. We need those who are different from us so we will be "better together."

The Apostle Paul describes the various gifts given to the body of Christ in his letter to the Corinthians, and concludes by saying:

If they were all one part, where would the body be? As it is, there are many parts, but one body.

—1 Corinthians 12:19–20

How true this is in marriage. The more we are able to fully appreciate the unique, different-from-us contribution our spouse makes, the better we are. As was mentioned earlier, I am the visionary, big-picture person; Virginia is the detailed, more "responsible" one. When we paint a room together, you are able to see how this works. I love the "big" jobs. I get the roller and go at it; no challenge is too big for me. I am not, however, inclined to do the detailed trim work and, left to myself, would leave the room unfinished. Virginia, on the other hand, loves to carefully paint the casework, baseboards, and fine window work, but would likely never start the room in the first place because she would be overwhelmed by the vastness of the job. When we appreciate our differences and work together, the room gets painted—because, in fact, we are "better together."

When we first got married, I thought the man was supposed to do the finances, so I balanced the checkbook and paid the bills— when I remembered them and could find them. Virginia would ask, "Did we pay our Visa bill?"

I would say, "I think so."

"Can you look and make sure?" she would reply.

"If I could find the checkbook and if I remembered to write it down—but don't worry, if I didn't pay the Visa bill, they'll just send another one next month!" Not an acceptable answer. *So*, Virginia does the checkbook and I tend to do the long-term investments.

The reason we own a couple of properties is because of my gifts as a visionary, whereas the reason we are not in jail is because Virginia is detailed and pays our bills. We are better off not trying to change each other into *our* image, but celebrating that the other has been created in *God's* image.

It is critical to realize that our differences are "hard wired" by God, and it is good. I do not leave staplers lying around because I want to upset Virginia; I do it because my mind has already "moved on." *Or,* as she says it, "Paul is never where he appears to be." This depersonalizes our differences, but is never an excuse for sin. I should always be seeking ways to be less irritating and more serving and accommodating to Virginia.

Remember that God created us male and female *before* the fall. All we have talked of thus far occurred before sin entered the world. We were created very differently and God said it was all *very good.* Our challenge as husbands and wives is to agree with Him.

God's design may be a bit mysterious, but it is perfect. When we start appreciating rather than critiquing our spouse, we will have made a giant step toward experiencing the intimacy God desires for us in marriage.

*When we put our spouse's needs above our own,
not only will they feel loved,
but it will propel our marriage towards greater intimacy.*

Reminders

☑ God's word is our "Operator's Manual."

☑ We have dignity as individuals created in the image of God.

☑ Just as the Trinity has diversity, being created in God's image makes us intentionally unique from each other.

☑ Our uniqueness as male and female is often seen in the areas of communication and sexuality.

☑ We are each "fearfully and wonderfully made" and are unique in our temperament wiring.

☑ We have the opportunity to either be frustrated by our uniqueness or look for ways it makes us "better together."

☑ God is the one who desires us to experience intimacy in marriage, and part of His plan includes making us different from each other: "and it was very good."

For Couples

Questions

1. What areas of your uniqueness have brought you the most joy in marriage?

2. What areas of your uniqueness have brought you the greatest challenges in marriage?

3. How can you see God's intentionally designing you uniquely making you "better together"?

APPlication

• Greet each other warmly when you awaken and when you pass each other during the day.

• Thank your spouse for a gift, ability, or character trait that you have little of and they have more of. Say something like "You are so good at _____. I sure am glad I am married to you!"

For Groups

1. What are some indicators of how fully we embrace God's word as our "Operator's Manual"?

2. Why is "reading the manual" such a challenge for us in marriage? What have you as individuals and as couples done to encourage each other to spend time regularly in God's word?

3. What are some of the most common ways we are tempted to not treat each other with dignity as spouses?

4. How might seeing God's design for diversity depersonalize some of the ways our gender or temperaments are an irritant to us?

5. Read Psalm 139:13–14. What do these verses highlight about each of us?

6. How might we affirm God's "fearfully and wonderfully made" creation of each other rather than trying to make our spouse more like ourselves?

7. How might Satan attempt to use our differences from each other to lead us away from each other rather than toward each other?

8. What does our culture say to do when we realize we are "just so different from our spouse?"

9. What ways can we follow God's manual rather than culture's when we are married to someone quite different from us?

Realize the enemy is not your spouse

"The thief comes only to steal and kill and destroy;
I have come that they may have life, and
have it to the full." —John 10:10

*I*f God is for marriage, Satan is against it. Genesis 3:1 says that the serpent was crafty.

Now the serpent was more crafty than any of the wild animals the LORD God had made. He said to the woman, "Did God really say, 'You must not eat from any tree in the garden'?"

—Genesis 3:1

Revelation 20:8 refers to Satan's goal to deceive the nations, and John 8:44 even says that Satan is the father of lies:

"You belong to your father, the devil, and you want to carry out your father's desire. He was a murderer from the beginning, not holding to the truth, for there is no truth in him. When he lies, he speaks his native language, for he is a liar and the father of lies." *—John 8:44*

Satan's goal is to "steal and kill and destroy." He will go to any lengths to hinder us from experiencing an intimate relationship with God and having life "to the full."

"The thief comes only to steal and kill and destroy; I have come that they may have life, and have it to the full." —John 10:10

Since marriage is one of God's primary avenues for passing on His values and His truths to the next generation, you can be sure Satan wants to bring down marriages as part of a larger effort to destroy families. Satan has painted a bull's-eye on the back of each marriage. Whether one is a follower of Christ or not, the covenant of marriage is God's idea. It is in the family that values are to be passed down, faith explained and demonstrated, love shown, and God's love modeled. Satan is fully aware that if he can take a marriage down, he affects the family; if he affects the family, it affects the church; if he affects the church, it will impact the community; if he can impact the community, he will affect the state; if he impacts the state, he affects the nation; and if he impacts the nation, he can affect the world.

Satan has painted a bull's-eye on the back of each marriage.

In this chapter we will look at various ways Satan attempts to use deception in order to disrupt the intimacy between God and man as well as between husband and wife. Deception, by its very definition, is intended to mislead. Deception is intended to cast doubt on that which is true. A false accusation that a pastor has had inappropriate affection for a parishioner (for example), though not true at all, may cast enough doubt to cause the church to suspect him and also bring about significant tension at home. Since Satan has nothing truthful to say about God that would hinder our relationship with Him, he simply plants deceptive seeds of doubt about God's plans for us, His goodness to us, and

His trustworthiness. In the area of marriage, Satan plants deceptive seeds of doubt about God's perfect plan for marriage and intimacy.

THE DECEPTION OF INDIVIDUALISM

It is interesting that in his first attempt to lure Adam and Eve away from God, Satan approached Eve separately. If God is for intimacy and oneness, you can be sure Satan will do all he can to separate and isolate couples from one another. That is why Satan and telemarketers have a lot in common: they both try to isolate before the sale. A telemarketer never says, "Before I try to sell you on my product, please ask your spouse to join you on the phone so you can decide together whether this would be the best way to spend your money as a couple." Similarly, Satan didn't ask Eve to consult Adam, "who was with her":

> *When the woman saw that the fruit of the tree was good for food and pleasing to the eye, and also desirable for gaining wisdom, she took some and ate it. She also gave some to her husband, who was with her, and he ate it.* —Genesis 3:6

Satan didn't say, "Eve, why don't you ask Adam what he thinks, since it was he to whom God gave the directions regarding what to eat and what not to eat?" Eve didn't stop to ask Adam either—she acted independently—nor did Adam involve himself and protect Eve. They each just did their own thing, and we have been paying for it ever since.

Satan has shown himself to be a master in using our culture to reinforce his plan to isolate and separate.

For some couples out of necessity, and for many out of personal desire, husbands and wives pursue their own vocations and no longer "need" each other. Daycare, nannies, and afterschool programs allow both parents to work full time and pursue their separate careers. Unfortunately, these dreams can end up as nightmares if people work so hard to realize their dreams that they lose sight of the spouses they originally meant to be part of the dream. Too many large houses never became homes, because no one is there.

There is no biblical argument against both husband and wife working, nor against pursuing personal dreams. However, we must guard against allowing selfish pursuits to threaten oneness in marriage. In Matthew 19, Jesus, when tested by the Pharisees about divorce, says, *". . . the two will become one . . . they are no longer two . . ."* This certainly does not mean that after two people are married they must no longer have any individual dreams, passions, talents, and hopes. What it does mean, however, is that each one's personal agenda must never hinder their marriage.

Bill sat bewildered in my office, describing his 15-year marriage. When he and his wife married, she was quite shy and withdrawn. She was insecure about her physical appearance and lacked confidence. Over the course of their marriage, Bill had tried to encourage his wife. She attended courses on public speaking, she cosmetically enhanced her body in a way that made her feel confident, and she landed a job that she was affirmed in. Before long she was excelling in her field and was asked to speak and travel. They both thought this was great, at first. Soon, however, she started traveling more and being home less, and finally asked for a divorce because her husband was not as exciting as the men she worked with. Satan won. He convinced her she really did not need her husband. She "found herself"—but lost her marriage.

I have always loved this quote by Mike Mason:

> A marriage is not a joining of two worlds, but an abandoning of two worlds in order that one new one might be formed.[9]

One of the things that normally draw couples together is their areas of common interests. More and more, however, we are seeing couples that are willing to, in essence, live parallel lives. They treat marriage as just one more thing they do, rather than a fundamentally different way of living. They have chemistry together and find this new addition to their life exciting, but believe it does not require them to give up anything they had as singles. So, the husband continues to go fishing every weekend and the wife hangs out with her friends and shops. And Satan wins, because the two never became one: they remain two, with "marriage" as just an add-on.

One of our single staff at the summer camp we direct told us about a female friend of his who was an avid hiker. They often hiked together and enjoyed the outdoors. He was a bit shocked when she announced she was marrying a computer nerd who thought the definition of hiking was walking from his desk to the refrigerator and back. Our friend challenged his hiking buddy about marrying someone who did not share her passion for hiking. "Oh, he's fine with me hiking without him, so nothing will change." A year later, our friend got a call from the young wife, begging him to go on an extended hike with him. "My husband will *never* hike with me. Please be my hiking partner." Fortunately our friend said, "No, you're married." But many others in similar situations have said yes and "hiked" into the sunset—with someone other than their spouse. See how crafty Satan is? He will lead us slowly away from our spouse, encouraging us to pursue our individual agenda, until we take a bite from the fruit and realize life has now drastically changed.

THE DECEPTION REGARDING GOD'S WORD

It is interesting that when Jesus is asked about relationships in Matthew 19, He says, "Haven't you read . . . ?" When Satan interacts with Eve in Genesis 3, he says, "Did God really say . . . ?"

The word of God is the authority on all matters for the Christian. Our view toward scripture will largely shape the decisions we make in life. Often scripture is portrayed as a book of don'ts that restrict people from fun and happiness. Nothing could be further from the truth. Scripture is the guide to abundant life, joy, and blessing. In fact, the word "blessed" is often translated "happy" and describes those who follow God's word. Psalm 1:1–2 describes the man as who follows God's ways as blessed or "happy":

> Blessed is the man
>> who does not walk in the counsel of the wicked
> or stand in the way of sinners
>> or sit in the seat of mockers.
> But his delight is in the law of the LORD,
>> and on his law he meditates day and night.
>
> —Psalm 1:1–2

The Psalmist encourages us to trust God and see how good He is:

> Taste and see that the LORD is good;
>> blessed is the man who takes refuge in him!
>
> —Psalm 34:8

God's intention is that His word would lead us to an abundant life in Him. Therefore, Satan will go to the greatest lengths to get God's people to doubt God's word. I am convinced it is our casual attitude toward the authority of God's word that is responsible for many of our marital and relational woes today. The paragraphs below list just a few of the areas in which Satan misleads couples, even when God's word is clear.

Whom to marry

An email I recently received stated, "I have a friend who is a strong Christian and she just got married . . . to an atheist. On top of the normal stresses of being newly married, she has now realized that not having a believer as a husband is a bigger deal than she originally thought. Any books you can recommend?"

I don't know—maybe the *Bible*? Just a thought. Perhaps if she had read 2 Corinthians 6:14: *"Do not be yoked together with unbelievers. For what do righteousness and wickedness have in common? Or what fellowship can light have with darkness?"* and followed it, she wouldn't be in the fix she is in now.

In the garden Satan said, "Did God really say . . . ?" and today he is doing the same, but in a more modern context. It goes like this: "What God really meant was to marry someone who brings you happiness."

Finances

Many couples are challenged when it comes to the area of finances and it becomes a source of significant tension. It often becomes an issue of right or wrong based on individual experiences or modeling from our families of origin. In our own case, Virginia came from a family that paid cash for everything. The only credit they had was the mortgage on their house.

God's intention is that His Word would lead us to an abundant life in Him.

If they didn't have the money for it, they didn't buy it. This certainly included items like clothing or eating out, but also larger-ticket items such as a washer/dryer or even a car. I, on the other hand, was raised on a farm, and we regularly took out loans to buy seeds or grain and to pay the bills connected with raising crops or animals. When the crops and animals were sold, the loans were repaid. Credit was a very good friend of ours.

Well, it doesn't take a rocket scientist to see what some of our early struggles were. For Virginia, if we don't have money, we don't go out to eat. For me, if we don't have money and we need to celebrate, we charge. In the end, we agreed that we could use credit cards, but never for more than we could pay off at the end of the month.

Fortunately for us, our positions on tithing were the same, since we both believed scripture alone should guide our giving decisions. However, this is not the case for all. A woman in a Bible study Virginia was leading, when asked about tithing, said the advice she had been given by one of her spiritual advisors was "It's like tipping at a restaurant. If the sermon is good, toss in a big bill; if the sermon is not so good, then don't give much." That made sense to this woman, but it does not square with scripture.

"Woe to you, teachers of the law and Pharisees, you hypocrites! You give a tenth of your spices—mint, dill and cummin. But you have neglected the more important matters of the law—justice, mercy and faithfulness. You should have practiced the latter, without neglecting the former." —Matthew 23:23

Jesus is saying it's no good to try to please God by tithing legalistically if you forget God's heart in pursuing justice, mercy, and faithfulness. On the other hand, he is *not* saying that your social concerns or emotions should replace your giving. He instructs us to practice justice, mercy, and faithfulness "without neglecting the former."

Too often, we live our life in a way that brings us what we want and often call our wants our needs—and then we say, at the end of the month, "we'd like to give more, but we just don't have the money." The principle in scripture is to give the Lord the best, the first 10%, and then work out your budget after that.

After 36 years of marriage, living on a single ministry salary for most of it, Virginia and I can say that we have lacked nothing, and God has met us in unbelievable ways. It really is best to trust Him with your finances. Someone once said to us that if you want to have financial "JOY," then give to Jesus first, Others second, and Yourself third. Solomon put it succinctly:

Honor the Lord with your wealth,
  with the firstfruits of all your crops;
then your barns will be filled to overflowing,
  and your vats will brim over with new wine.
My son, do not despise the Lord's discipline
  and do not resent his rebuke.   —*Proverbs 3:9–11*

This area can cause great conflict if the couples' convictions are not based on scripture and are not shared.

Language

The couple in our office could not have been meaner to each other. They put each other down and pointed out each other's faults. If only their mate would be different, the whole marriage would be fine. They used language that was degrading and, frankly, crude.

Do not let any unwholesome talk come out of your mouths, but only what is helpful for building others up according to their needs, that it may benefit those who listen.   —*Ephesians 4:29*

We are instructed to speak in a wholesome manner to our spouse, using only words that benefit and build up our spouse. But the deceiver says, "Get it off your chest, be authentic, don't hold back, you'll feel better."

Media

A man was trying to convince his wife that looking at pornography would be fine, since they were watching it together and it would improve their sex life.

But among you there must not be even a hint of sexual immorality, or of any kind of impurity, or of greed, because these are improper for God's holy people.   —*Ephesians 5:3*

We are to fill our minds only with that which brings honor to God and encourages us to treat our spouse with honor as well.

Satan would say, "Whatever gives you better sex is what God would want for you—after all, He created it!"

Truthfulness

A husband explained to us that it was more loving to not always be honest with his wife. "For instance," he said, "she doesn't want me drinking beer with the guys, so I tell her I'm working late. That way I don't make her upset."

Therefore each of you must put off falsehood and speak truthfully to his neighbor, for we are all members of one body.
—Ephesians 4:25

Scripture is very clear that we are to be truthful to each other. Here Satan very cleverly twists other scriptural principles to tempt us to disobedience. He says, "Being loving is the most important thing, and telling the truth might hurt your spouse, so it really is more loving to lie occasionally."

Sexual purity

Virginia received an email from a woman who was unhappy with her life. She said she and her husband had nothing in common, and she felt she was missing out on life because of being married to him. I asked Virginia, "Why did she marry him in the first place?" She was pregnant, was the reason given. Satan is so conniving! He entices us to follow our hormones in one area of disobedience to God's word, and then wreaks havoc in many other areas of our lives.

It is God's will that you should be sanctified: that you should avoid sexual immorality; that each of you should learn to control his own body in a way that is holy and honorable, not in passionate lust like the heathen, who do not know God;
—1 Thessalonians 4:3–5

If the GPS keeps telling you to go south and you go north, don't be upset with the GPS when you end up in South Dakota rather than Southern Florida! God is not against us being happy, but He *is* against us being disobedient to His word in order to obtain "happiness." The fact is, happiness will never be found when we disobey God. Disobedience ultimately robs God of the glory He deserves and robs us of the joy that we are looking for.

THE DECEPTION THAT CHARACTER IS IMPORTANT ONLY WHEN PEOPLE ARE LOOKING

Committed adherence to God's word leads to character in everyday life. Satan hates men and women of conviction because they make character decisions that lead toward health and righteousness.

We met with a Christian couple in which the husband had just had an affair. The wife was screaming at her husband, "How could you do this to me? What got into you? I can't understand you leaving me for another woman!" After what seemed to be an appropriate time,

> *Disobedience ultimately robs God of the glory He deserves and robs us of the joy we are looking for.*

we said to her, "You should have *some* sense of understanding, since you were the woman who broke up his first marriage. Why did you think a man of no character in his first marriage would become a man of character in his second marriage?" (Obviously, a genuine encounter with Christ could change one's character, but in this case, both parties professed Christ.)

Scripture must always overrule our hormones. When we teach Christian engaged couples, we always point out, "If you are sleeping with each other now, there is no reason to believe your spouse won't commit adultery after marriage." We are not saying they will, but there is no reason for them not to. If they allowed their hormones to overrule scripture before they are married, there is no way to be confident they will each make sure scripture over-rules their hormones after they are married.

Satan wants us to believe that scripture gives us suggestions to ponder, not commands to obey. He wants us to believe God's word is outdated. But God's word must be our final authority over emotions, hormones, and cultures.

THE DECEPTION OF HAPPINESS

When the woman saw that the fruit of the tree was good for food and pleasing to the eye, and also desirable for gaining wisdom, she took some and ate it. She also gave some to her husband, who was with her, and he ate it. —Genesis 3:6

You can't imagine how many times the word "happy" is used in our counseling office, given most that people who come in are generally unhappy. (It's rare that a couple books an appointment with us to say they are happy and just wanted to drop in and let us know.)

Men will often say to me, "Don't I have the right to be happy?" I reply, "No: you're married." Of course, I'm joking—but seriously, who said we had the right to be happy? What about the respon-sibility to do the right thing for those we say we love? We have opportunities to honor God and our mate, to strive to be the men and women God has called us to be, and to serve others and put their interests above our own. But to have our personal happiness as our "right"? I don't think so. Happiness isn't a right—rather, it is a by-product of deep intimacy with God and service to others.

June was unhappy in her marriage, telling us that her husband did not give her the attention she deserved. June's male co-worker was married to a woman who did not meet his "needs." Before long, June and Bill shared their stories of misery over lunch. Three months later, they were sharing their stories in bed. June claimed her co-workers said she deserved to be happy and if Bill made her happy and connected with her in a way that her husband didn't, then who would blame her for leaving him . . . and her three children?

Sally came into my office at the church to get my "pastoral blessing" on her divorce.

"On what grounds are you divorcing your husband," I asked. "Is he unfaithful to you?"

"Oh, no," she said.

"Does he physically abuse you?"

"Not at all."

"Does he fail to provide for your financially?"

"Oh, no, he provides very well."

"Is he an unfit parent?"

"No, and that's the worst part—the children will miss him terribly."

"I am sorry," I responded, "then what is the reason you are leaving your husband?"

"He's boring!" was her response.

"Okay," I replied, "let me see whether 'boring' is in the list of acceptable biblical reasons for divorce . . ." (Nope.)

I in no way want to minimize the fact that some marriages are not what we had dreamed of or hoped for. I am certainly not saying we are to stay in marriages where there is repeated, unrepentant infidelity or where there is desertion or abuse. I am saying that simple lack of "happiness" is not a reason to leave the marriage. If it were, we would always be tempted to see if an "upgrade" were possible with another person.

> If the purpose of marriage was simply to enjoy an infatu-
> ation and make me "happy," then I'd have to get a "new"
> marriage every two or three years. But if I really wanted
> to see God transform me from the inside out, I'd need to
> concentrate on changing *myself* rather than on changing
> my *spouse*.[10]

Studies actually show that those who leave unhappy marriages to "find happiness" are less likely to find it than those who stay married.

> According to the survey, conducted by a team of family researchers, unhappily married adults who divorced were no happier five years after the divorce than were equally unhappy marrieds who remained together. And two-thirds of unhappily married people who remained married reported that their marriages were happy five years later. Even among those who had rated their marriages as "very unhappy", nearly 80 percent said they were happily married five years later. These were not merely bored or dissatisfied whiners. They had endured serious problems, including alcoholism, infidelity, verbal abuse, emotional neglect, depression, illness, and work and money troubles.
>
> Even more surprising, unhappy spouses who divorced actually showed slightly more depressive symptoms five years later than those who didn't. . . .
>
> But the most telling aspect of this research is the light it sheds on the importance of the attitude toward marriage. Those who enter marriage with a dim (some might say accurate) view of divorce and a strong religious or other motivation for avoiding it are not only less likely to divorce, they are also less likely to be unhappy. That is the arresting news here. We've known that commitment was good for the children of such marriages. And we've known that commitment was good for society. But until now, it was not clear that commitment actually made married couples themselves more likely to be happy.[11]

Satan says, "Pursue happiness, you deserve it." God says, "Pursue me and a life that honors me, and blessing and happiness will follow." True happiness comes in marriage when we treasure Christ above all else and when we become more Christ-like in serving our spouse. You want to be happy in your marriage? Great! But happiness isn't going to come by jumping ship or by being self-serving. Happiness will come in your marriage when you are faithful to your commitment and when you follow the example of Christ in selflessness. This is the irony of intimacy.

THE DECEPTION OF NO CONSEQUENCE

"You will not surely die," the serpent said to the woman. "For God knows that when you eat of it your eyes will be opened, and you will be like God, knowing good and evil."
—Genesis 3:4–5

When I was a boy, we were told that smoking would kill you, but I saw lots of guys at school smoking and they were playing sports, were popular, had girlfriends, and went out on more dates than I did. I guess those who told us bad things about cigarettes were liars! Well, not exactly. Satan's lie is that "if bad things don't happen immediately, they won't happen at all."

Adam and Eve ate the fruit, and did not die . . . that day. But they eventually did die physically; worse yet, they became spiritually dead and were alienated from God.

Lilly joined a bicycle club and loved riding. Before long, riding became her life. On one ride, she met a man who enjoyed riding with her. Before long, they were riding off alone and thought riding off into the sunset would bring them both happiness. Lilly decided she needed to be "true to her heart" and left her husband and family.

Eventually Lilly became convicted that leaving her family had been wrong. Because she was a "strong Christian," she decided to leave her riding friend and return home to her "forgiving family." It took a while, but the marriage and family started to be repaired.

Part of the new agreement between Lilly and her husband and children was a "no tolerance" position: if she returned to her riding partner again, the marriage was over.

She did really well for a while, but then met up with him again.

Lilly now weeps; she is all alone. Her children will not speak to her, her marriage has ended, and she cannot believe that she has lost everything dear to her. She bought Satan's lie that you can always go back and everything will be fine again.

The reason we set such strict safeguards around marriage is that Satan has the ability to blind us to what the consequences of our actions will be. It is almost as though once we take that decisive step against God's word, we cannot see more than five minutes ahead. We fail to see that momentary pleasure will bring a lifetime of undesirable consequences.

Proverbs 6 states clearly that we cannot be unfaithful to our marriage vows without consequences:

> *Can a man scoop fire into his lap*
> *without his clothes being burned?*
> *Can a man walk on hot coals*
> *without his feet being scorched?*
> *So is he who sleeps with another man's wife;*
> *no one who touches her will go unpunished.*
> —*Proverbs 6:27–29*

I will never forget the summer one of our staff came to camp and, when asked how he was doing, said "They lied to me. All the people who gave their testimonies at camp and church lied to me. They said they had lived a life of blatant sin, but had asked Christ to forgive them, and now everything is great." He went on to say that he had always tried to follow Christ and avoid sin. Finally, after listening to testimony after testimony, he thought to himself, "Why should I be missing out on partying, sex, drinking, and the rest? I'll do it for a while and then ask for forgiveness." With tears he said, "I know what I did was wrong. I have asked forgiveness, and I know I am forgiven—but life is not great. I have a sexually transmitted disease that will go with me all the days of my life. I violated women, I hurt my parents, I hurt my Christian witness, and all is not great."

Satan wants us to believe that we can ignore God for now, and later seek forgiveness as our ticket to "happiness" without consequences. Perhaps no greater lie has ever been told.

THE DECEPTION OF GREATER SATISFACTION

Satan has a way of taking what God has given and convincing us he can improve on it. I have struggled my whole life with weight control; some would say I have not struggled enough. I have what I call half of an eating disorder: I binge but I don't purge. Over the course of my life I have lost over a thousand pounds, but I have managed to find them all again. One of the best programs I followed, however, was the Zone eating plan. I lost a good deal of weight and felt great; some even said I looked great. But then one day I thought, "If the Zone plan is so good, I bet the Zone plus Snickers would be even better." So I "improved" on the plan and enlarged my waistline.

God is the one that has given us the "perfect program," and yet we so often listen to Satan, who offers to "improve" on the plan. "Marriage is great, but marriage plus a little porn will be even better," he whispers. "Marriage is great, but putting my children ahead of my husband will be even better," he suggests. "Marriage is great, but flirting around with others will add to my happiness," he tempts.

Jill and Joe met with us after the discovery that Joe had been in a six-month affair with a woman in his company. After trying to reconcile, but not cutting off relationship with his mistress, Joe sat his wife and four children down and told them he was leaving them and moving in with Rachael.

When I asked him why he was leaving, he said his wife was controlling and he was no longer happy in his home. Life in every arena was routine. But when he and Rachael met for coffee, it was exciting; when they went on trips, it was light and fun; and when they had sex, it was like it was before he was married.

Three days after moving in with Rachael, Joe was back in my office. "I want to go back to my wife and family," he said. "I just made the worst mistake of my life."

"Why the quick change?" I asked.

"Well," he said, "I moved in on Friday, and Sunday morning we were in the kitchen having coffee and she was telling me I needed to take out the garbage and 'please don't leave your dishes lying around, I'm not a maid, you know.'" Joe told me he woke up and thought, "This is no different from what I had at home, except that now I have lost my children and wife." The illicit may seem tantalizing, but only for a season.

Following Satan's lead will always lead to the destruction of God's perfect design for marriage.

> *With persuasive words she led him astray;*
> *she seduced him with her smooth talk.*
> *All at once he followed her*
> *like an ox going to the slaughter,*
> *like a deer stepping into a noose*
> *till an arrow pierces his liver,*
> *like a bird darting into a snare,*
> *little knowing it will cost him his life.*
> —*Proverbs 7:21–23*

I will never forget meeting with a man after he ended an affair with a woman. He read the above passage to me and said, "That was me." How true scripture is!

And, oh, how the illicit entices! The illicit will always trump the legitimate in excitement and thrill. Why else would men and women leave the security of a relationship to risk it all for a night of sin?

God has given us the ability to experience sexual pleasure. He has drawn a boundary around sexual stimulation and set it in a very special place: to be experienced only within marriage. Satan can't top sex, so he attempts to convince us that he can give it to us outside of God's boundaries. He attempts to convince us that casual sex is thrilling without the responsibility of marriage.

> *The illicit may seem tantalizing, but only for a season.*

The problem with Satan's plan is that it doesn't work. Casual sex is still sex—and sex is designed to be experienced only within the marriage relationship. Even an atheist gets uptight when his/her "significant other" gets involved sexually with someone other than himself or herself.

Remember that Satan's *only* goal is to "steal and kill and destroy." He has *no* interest in your pleasure other than to use it to lure you away from God's design for you. Satan wants us to believe that by following God we will miss out on so much excitement, fun, and life. But that's not so. We too often stress only the negative ramifications of disobedience to God: pregnancy, sexuality transmitted disease, alcoholism, children damaged through divorce, etc. Instead, we should stress not what will go wrong, but all that you will miss out on.

On a recent flight, I sat next to a 21-year-old girl from a very dysfunctional home; when she was 15, her family disintegrated, and she was left to live on her own. As I heard her story, I just could not stop thinking of all the experiences in life her mom and dad were missing out on. She had not talked to her mom in years and no longer had any relationship with her dad. Her dad and mom had missed out on vacationing together as a family, on sitting together at her graduation; they will miss walking her down the aisle at her wedding, being there to hold her first child, seeing their granddaughter's first recital—and the list goes on.

The last verse of Genesis 2 states that Adam and Eve were "both naked, and they felt no shame." In Genesis 3:1, Satan shows up, saying he can improve on God's plan by adding a bit of zest. Look

> *It is Satan who is the real enemy in marriage, not one another.*

at the end of Chapter 3 after Satan has "improved" everything. Instead of being naked and unashamed, Adam and Even are now separated from each other and hiding from God.

Satan has no new plays. He is still attempting to entice us not to trust God and instead to believe that he can improve on God's plan.

God loves us and truly wants the best for each of us individually, in our marriage, and for our family. We will miss out when we choose not to follow the Lord.

At the end of the day it is important to remember that it is Satan who is the real enemy in marriage, not one another. Satan uses us against each other effectively at times, but it is all part of his strategy to "steal and kill and destroy" our marriages, our relationship with God, and us!

THE DECEPTION THAT OUR SPOUSE SHOULD MEET ALL OUR NEEDS

This deception is especially rampant in the Christian community. We talk about our "better half" and being married to our "soul mate." We search for "the one who will complete us."

When Virginia and I were dating, I would look for cards to

send her. Many had sentiments such as "The sky was gray until I met you," "The flowers never bloomed until we were together," and "The grass was always brown before we met" (the kind you mowed). These and many other slogans implied that one is not complete until one is married.

The flaw in this, of course, is thinking that one's completion or happiness is dependent on another person. If you think so, you will have a tendency to place high demands on them to assure your happiness.

I love what Larry Crabb says:

> Because we are not experiencing the satisfaction that comes from resting in God's goodness, we look to our partners to meet our needs. When they fail to do so, as inevitably they will, we retreat behind protective distance to minimize our discomfort. But, because we are "Bible-believing Christians," we nobly carry on with the responsibilities of marriage in a spirit of obedient martyrdom, persuaded that God admires our devotion to duty.[12]

Most Christian men today would suggest that Billy Graham is about as closely connected to God as anyone can be—and yet even his wife stated that Billy was not enough:

> It is a foolish woman who expects her husband to be to her that which only Jesus Christ Himself can be: always ready to forgive, totally understanding, unendingly patient, invariably tender and loving, unfailing in every area, anticipating every need, and making more than adequate provision. Such expectations put a man under an impossible strain. The same goes for the man who expects too much from his wife.[13]

When we see our first priority as developing intimacy with Christ, even above intimacy with our spouse, the result is a life reflecting God's image more fully and thus being the spouse we are called to be and experiencing the intimacy we have always longed for more fully. When we experience such intimacy with Christ, we then long to serve our spouse in such a way that they experience this intimacy as well. Hear Larry Crabb again:

> If I have experienced the answer to my deepest longings in Christ, then I will be able to see past my longings and discern my wife's needs; and when I see her needs, then my experience of satisfaction with Christ will create in me a deep desire to promote similar satisfaction in my wife.[14]

THE TRUTH: YOU ARE A TEAM! YOU WIN OR LOSE AS A TEAM

It was the first Superbowl after 9/11. Emotions were running high as the Saint Louis Rams were introduced to a frenzied crowd at the Louisiana Superdome in New Orleans. It was now time for the New England Patriots to be introduced, and for superstars such as Tom Brady to be introduced individually. But instead of introducing star after star, the announcer simply said, "representing the AFC, the New England Patriots," and

If one wins, both win; if one loses, both lose.

they came out as a team. There were no individual introductions. And they won—as a team.

In marriage, since the two become one, there really is no individual winning or losing. If one wins, both win; if one loses, both lose. It is impossible for one spouse to win and the other spouse to lose. It may seem like a silly example, but imagine two superstars playing on the same basketball team. Both individuals are excellent players and very competitive. The game is tied and only a few seconds remain on the clock. One player has the ball and is heading for the game-winning basket when he is knocked to the floor—not by the opponent, but by his teammate, who wants to be the one to score the winning basket! The game is over, their team lost, and the superstars both lost. Sometimes it seems almost that ridiculous in marriage. Instead of looking for ways to "pass off the ball" so our teammate has a good shot, we hog the ball and shoot it ourselves so as to be the stars, even though the team suffers for it.

The opposing team is Satan. He needs no help! We must play our best game together to defeat him—for our own sake, for the sake of the team, and for the glory of our Owner!

*W*hen we put our spouse's needs above our own,
not only will they feel loved,
but it will propel our marriage towards greater intimacy.

Reminders

☑ Since oneness in marriage is so critical to God's design for mankind, Satan is working overtime to do all he can to isolate us from one another.

☑ Our culture encourages individual pursuits more than marital unity.

☑ Pursuing one's individual interests often leads to parallel lives.

☑ Satan does all he can to discredit scripture, constantly asking us if God really means what it seems He says.

☑ Our culture has bought into Satan's lie that everything is acceptable as long as it brings personal happiness.

☑ Satan wants us to believe that you can sin and then ask God's forgiveness, without there being any lasting consequences.

☑ One of Satan's biggest lies is that he can improve what God has for us.

☑ We are a team and must play not as individuals, but *for* each other and *against* our opponent, Satan.

For Couples

Questions

1. Which of the seven deceptions do you feel you have struggled with the most in your marriage?

2. How practically can you recognize that Satan is the enemy of your marriage, not each other, and fight against him?

APPlication

+ Commit to doing something together this week that you often "divide and conquer."

+ As a couple, make an appointment with a couple married longer than you that you respect, and together ask them five questions regarding what has contributed to the health of their marriage.

For Groups

1. Read Malachi 2:13–16.

    • What does this passage say about the "craftiness" of the evil one to lure us away from God's purposes for marriage?

2. How have you seen the deception of individualism affect marriages today?

3. In what ways does Satan plant the "Did God really say?" question in marriages today?

4. Of the areas listed in which scripture and culture conflict, which ones do you feel causes the most tension in marriages today?

5. How can churches more effectively counter the lie that divorce will not have lasting affects, without heaping unnecessary guilt on those who are divorced?

6. What is it that tempts us to feel that life might be better if we were not married, or if we were married to someone else?

7. Why, with statistics and experience with broken relationships being so dismal, is Satan still scoring so many "victories" against God's design for marriage?

5

> *". . . 'For this reason a man will leave his father and*
> *mother and be united to his wife, and the two will*
> *become one flesh'? So they are no longer two, but*
> *one flesh. Therefore what God has joined together,*
> *let man not separate."* —Matthew 19:5–6

*W*ho could have imagined, back on their wedding day, that one would have to be intentional about making marriage a priority? After all, we "fell in love," and intimacy came so naturally that it all seemed easy. We always wanted to be with each other, share fully with each other, affirm each other, cuddle with each other, and then it happened . . . Marriage.

But just as a house without maintenance deteriorates, so a marriage without the priority of intentional care quickly starts to crumble. More houses are destroyed by termites—which, gone untreated, eat at the structural elements of the house while the outside continues to look just fine—than by earthquakes, hurricanes, or tornadoes. Most houses that deteriorate don't collapse from a catastrophic event but from a lifetime of neglect. And so it is with marriages.

A family moved into our neighborhood about 10 years ago and purchased a house very similar to ours. They have regularly maintained their house and have added a front porch, solar heating, and new siding, among other improvements. Their house has increased in appearance and value since they moved in. Our house, on the other hand, not so much. These two houses are apt metaphors for this chapter. After we get married, we have the choice to maintain and improve our marriage, or to do nothing and wonder why it seems to be deteriorating.

THE PRIORITY OF MARRIAGE

The critical importance of making marriage a top priority should come as no surprise. One of the first directives to Adam and Eve regarded "leaving" father and mother in order to make the marriage relationship a top priority.

For this reason a man will leave his father and mother and be united to his wife, and they will become one flesh.
—*Genesis 2:24*

Now, Adam and Eve themselves had no father or mother, but don't let that derail you from this incredibly important commandment regarding marriage that God is giving to the first couple. He is already helping them understand their role in the lives of their children. They are not to become "one" with their children, but are to prepare their children to eventually leave them and "become one" with someone else.

In the course of a marriage, there are many things that will vie for priority. Many of these are actually good things, but when put before the marriage become out of balance.

PRIORITY OVER PARENTS

The Hebrew word translated here as "leave" literally means to "cut, sever, abandon." This does not mean that you should sever all relationships with your parents, but it does mean that you are to sever your primary allegiance with your parents and establish it with your spouse.

Virginia and I signed a contract to buy our first house on the day after we were married. It was 1976 in Southern California, and real estate prices were starting to take off. Given our take-home ministry salary of $600 per month, the only way we could qualify for a mortgage was to accept an interest-only loan, with a balloon payment due in 10 years. We talked to our folks about it, and Virginia's mom and dad reminded us that they had saved for 10 years before buying their own house. Virginia's dad told us very specifically that he thought we were very unwise to do what we were doing. Instead, he thought we should rent, save, and buy later. Virginia and I listened to him, talked together, and then Virginia thanked him for his advice, but said we had decided to buy the house. She had successfully "left" her parents. If she had not left, she would have most likely said, "Paul, you are 25 years old and you have never bought a house. My dad has purchased many and understands finances way more than you. I am not going to sign those papers unless my dad approves." Virginia didn't sever her relationship with her parents, but she had switched her primary allegiance to me, and we, together, made the decision.

Fortunately, the market did take off and that purchase was our best investment ever.

I have been fortunate enough to co-officiate at two of our daughters' weddings to date. Each time, I said to the bride during the ceremony, "In about twenty minutes you will be pronounced husband and wife. From that time on, you have no obligation to do anything I say. I will no longer be your primary male advisor–your husband is to have that role."

When we spoke in Uganda on God's design for marriag⸠ received this question: "My husband's relatives are ruini⸍ marriage. They have taken everything that I have. My ⸍ listens more to his relatives than to me. I am only seen a⸍ to him. I have no happiness at all. Please advise."

No matter where in the world we speak, the issue of parents and in-laws is an issue. As we said in answer to her question, whenever culture and scripture collide, scripture must prevail. Scripture is clear that after marriage the primary unit is the marriage, not the extended family. It also says that we are to care for our family. This can be a tension after marriage. Our parents are no longer to direct our lives, yet we are always to strive for a harmonious relationship of love and care for them.

The biggest challenges involving "leaving" one's parents and "being united" to one's spouse often occur around holiday time. There are often high expectations that holiday traditions will continue as always, simply with the addition of another place setting at the holiday table. I certainly am not against being with parents during the holidays, but the critical issue is that the decisions on where to be, when to be, and with whom to be should be the decisions of the newlywed couple, not their parents.

I was told about a couple celebrating their first married Christmas. The bride was excited to start their own traditions and was shocked when her husband said he wanted to spend Christmas Eve at his mom's house and sleep in his old room so he could wake up in his own bed like it always had been at Christmas. The new wife listened and then simply said, "Not if you want to see me naked again."

To repeat, "leave" means to "cut, sever, abandon." You are not being grafted into the family tree, you are a new sapling. Sometimes a young couple will say to us, "We want to leave, but our parents won't let go." Note that the scripture passage doesn't say "For this reason, the parents will let go . . . ." It says, "For this reason a man will leave . . . ." The responsibility to put your marriage first is yours.

According to scripture, as an adult you are called to honor your parents; only children are called to obey them.

A mom may enjoy the experience of pregnancy and wish that

her baby could always have its needs met simply through the umbilical cord, but unless the cord is cut and the baby is able to function independently from his or her mother, that baby will never grow to be an adult. So it is in marriage. Parents may love the memories of their nuclear family and of caring for their children, but unless they "cut the cord," their children will never be able to function fully as adults.

PRIORITY OVER CHILDREN

In America, we live in a child-centered culture. A few weeks ago, we met with a couple where the husband expressed concern that he and his wife were "drifting apart" and seldom had any time to connect. The wife blurted out, "Well, get used to it. This is the 21st century and you have to have your kids in ballet, gymnastics, music, and soccer. That is just the way it is."

Husband – Wife
DIAGRAM #1

Husband – Child – Wife
DIAGRAM #2

When a couple first gets married, their lives are like diagram #1, both overlapping each other. They have separate interests, but plenty of shared time and space. Then, they have a child. I can distinctly remember trying to hug and kiss Virginia and having one of our three daughters attempt to wiggle her way in between us. I love my girls, but they were never designed to come between us as husband and wife.

Over the course of time, our lives may come to be more represented by diagram #2, where the main things that connect us are the children. Our conversations are about the children, our meals out are with the children, our vacations are with the children. In the last two months alone, I have heard of two different couples who are taking their children to Hawaii for their 25th wedding anniversary. Something feels wrong with that to me. Anniversaries are opportunities to get away as a couple, take walks on the beach, have long uninterrupted conversations, have romantic dinners together, sleep in, run around naked together, and have raucous sex—not to spend time with your children!

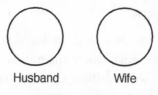

Husband   Wife

DIAGRAM #3

When the children leave home, they drop out of the diagram, and unless you have stayed connected as a couple, it is easy to find yourselves looking at each other and asking, "Who are *you*?" The empty nest is statistically one of the highest times for divorce. Diagram #3 demonstrates visually what too many couples experience after the children leave home.

It is reported that Dr. John Rosemond, world-renowned psychologist and parenting expert, was once asked by a young couple attending his marriage seminar to give them his best advice on parenting. "Gladly," he responded. "Work on your marriage." The young couple told him they appreciated that but actually wanted to know what to do in regards to parenting. "You heard me correctly: work on your marriage," he responded. Christian and secular counselors alike agree that the best gift a couple can give their children is a stable marriage.

I will never forget meeting with a couple in which the man worked for a start-up company. He was away from home Monday through Friday and worked from home on the weekends. His upset wife said, "You have left me for your start-up company. I feel all alone, abandoned, and not a priority for you." After a bit, he said quietly, "Now I guess you know what I feel like." She quickly snapped back, "I have never worked outside the home." "True enough," he said, "but five years ago we had our first child and you left me for the children. I have felt all alone, abandoned, and not a priority for you." Jobs are good, and children are a gift from God, but Satan is able to use both to distance us from each other if we are not intentional. Scripture says *"the two will become one,"* not the three, four, or five. We are to love our children, but they are not to come before our marriage relationship.

It is ironic that many couples both work so that their children can attend private schools, take ballet, be on traveling sports teams, live in the big house, take great vacations, etc., only to drift apart and hurt their children far more than forgoing all the above would, because their marriage fell apart.

We recently met with a couple that have three children. The wife spends 5 hours a night doing homework with the children. The couple have not been out on a date for years because the wife "can't leave the kids . . ."

Another couple came in because they were ready to divorce. In the course of the counseling session, we heard them say that their children, ages 2 and 4, stayed up until 11 pm each night. We helped them to adjust the bedtime to 8 pm. The second counseling session ended up focused again on parenting and not on their marriage. At our third meeting, we started the session by saying, "Let's talk about your marriage tonight."

"Why?" they asked. "We are doing great!" All they had needed was a little more sleep and time together.

We have some dear friends who for their entire marriage have had Thursday night as their date night. When their children complained and whined about them going out they always explained, "This is important for mommy and daddy so our marriage stays strong and we continue to enjoy each other and be better parents."

One Thursday, our friends were having a particularly rough day with each other. They were short with each other and were taking their emotions out on the kids, as well. Late in the afternoon, one of their young daughters asked the dad if they were going on their date night. "Yes—why do you ask?" he inquired. "Good, because you sure need it!" was her reply.

Be intentional about getting away for a weekend together, have regular date nights, and don't let your young children stay up late and eat into your couple time. *You* are the parents.

We have three children. We love children and we love being with our children, but they were never designed to come before our marriage relationship.

PRIORITY IN ALL DECISIONS

The principle God has laid down as a framework for marriage is critical for us to understand and we believe is at the root of much of our marital distress today. You will never be able to "be one" and experience deep intimacy with your spouse until you readjust your priorities.

When Jesus said, *"the two will become one . . . they are no longer two,"* He was explaining that marriage is a paradigm shift, not an add-on to our single lives. The two become one, *they are no longer two!* This does not mean we no longer have our own individual gifts, abilities, passions, and dreams. But it does mean that from this time on, all our decisions must go through the "marriage grid." Does this strengthen or weaken my marriage? I may have a job opportunity that I have always dreamed of, but it will take me away from my wife and family. If, indeed, it will hinder my marriage and family, I must say no. I don't have a covenant relationship with my dreams; I do with my wife. Perhaps a wife has a passion for public education but realizes it's consuming her time to the point of neglecting her marriage and family. She must curtail or eliminate her work if it hinders her relationship with her husband and family.

Virginia's father always dreamed of being a pilot. He was elated when he was selected to be a Navy pilot. Virginia's mom and dad had three children age 3 and under during the time they were living in Florida, while he was in training to be a Navy pilot. Within a span of one week, three planes went down, killing the pilots. Virginia's mom said she didn't think she could live this way, with the constant worry for her husband's safety, knowing she had three young children to raise and a fourth on the way. After they talked about it, Dad asked for a transfer out of pilot training—not because he loved flying any less, but because he loved Mom more and had made a covenant commitment to her. This should have been the kiss of death for his aspirations to rise in rank as a naval officer. But God honored his decision, and Dad was a Rear Admiral when he retired from his navy career—and he has just celebrated 64 years of marriage with Mom.

> *The two will become one ... they are no longer two.*

We met with a doctor and his wife for marriage counseling. As a surgeon, he needed to leave each morning before 6 am and did not return home most nights until after 9 pm. The wife said this schedule was extremely stressful to their marriage. But her husband replied, "I didn't work this long to give up surgery. If you don't like it, you can leave. I can always find a new wife, but I won't give up being a doctor."

Contrast this with a friend of ours who was told he was in line for the VP position in his company. If he would stay later each night and work the weekends, he would be a shoo-in. "Then I guess I won't be a VP," he said, "since I have a wife and four children to whom I have a greater commitment."

Another couple came to us because she owned dogs that slept with them each night—*big* dogs. Her husband said he just couldn't take it any longer. She countered, "You knew I had dogs." "Not in bed with us," he replied. It was him or the dogs, and she chose the dogs.

When our oldest daughter, Kari, gave birth to our first grandchild, a boy, Brandon was the major focus of all of our attention. When he was first born, Kari gave Brandon way more attention than she did her husband, Gabe. That was to be expected and was certainly needed during the time of transition into parenthood. Does this mean that Kari no longer has given Gabe exclusive ranking as her #1 commitment? Certainly not. There are definitely periods in our lives when we must give most (or all) of our attention somewhere else. This does not mean we no longer love our spouse. But if, four years later, Kari is still paying more attention to this little guy and his needs than to her husband, there would be reason for concern. The marriage relationship is to take precedence over all other relationships, even children.

The marriage relationship is to take precedence over all other relationships, even children.

The examples could go on and on, but I think you get the drift. The marriage must be the priority. It is a discipline to put the marriage first at times, because it may not be what we "want" to do. But as Virginia always says, it is a lot easier to act your way into a new way of feeling than to feel your way into a new way of acting.

You have a covenant relationship with God and your spouse—with nothing else and with no one else.

PRIORITY OF EXCLUSIVE RELATIONSHIPS

We have addressed the priority of marriage over work, hobbies, family, children, church, etc. But now we focus on its exclusive nature.

There are only two exclusive relationships we are to have: our relationship with Christ, and our relationship with our spouse.

The first commandment says, "You may have *no* other gods before me." This does not mean God must be first, ahead of the close second. It means rather that there are *no other gods.* Scripture says it is *impossible* to serve two masters. When Christ calls us to follow Him, He asks for complete allegiance and an exclusive relationship.

> *Then he said to them all: "If anyone would come after me, he must deny himself and take up his cross daily and follow me."*
> —Luke 9:23

We are called to abandon all that would impede complete devotion to our triune God. God is not saying that He wants to be first in the running with many gods; there are to be no other gods. Just as we are not to have other gods before God, we are not to put any other person before our spouse. Virginia is not amused if I tell her, as we drift off to sleep, "I love you more than all the other women I love." She doesn't want to be the first of many. She expects, and rightly so, to be my one and only.

Because the marriage relationship is to be exclusive, we must guard it with all our heart. We are to let nothing come in that would eat away at the vitality of our relationship. Every time Virginia and I counsel someone who has had an affair, that person can pinpoint the time when their relationship crossed the "exclusive" line and they started sharing with another what was only to be shared with their spouse.

We often hear a counselee state that his or her affair was "an accident." But the only affair that is an accident is if two people are walking down the sidewalk naked and they bump into each other. Every other affair is intentional. You may say, "Not so, it was an accident that I started to like her!" It may not have been intentional at first, but early on you surely knew it was not right—and from that time you were intentional about when you took your break, where you went for lunch, what you didn't tell your spouse, and so on.

Here is the simplest way we can put it: If you are married and you start finding increasing enjoyment in the company of someone of the opposite sex other than your spouse, you need to end that relationship or curtail it significantly. It may be a co-worker with whom you have coffee, or a friend with whom you chat at the children's bus stop, or your best friend's spouse with whom you vacation. Whoever it is, you need to stop the relationship.

Jim and Jane had friends with whom they vacationed and whom they invited over to their house frequently, as their girls loved being together. As time went on, Jim started enjoying hanging out and talking with Barbara, Jane's best friend. Since everyone trusted everyone, no one thought much about it when Barbara and Jim started to stay up after their spouses went to bed while on vacation, since they were the night owls in the bunch. Now they are both divorced. There came a time early in the relationship when both Jim and Barbara knew they were starting to have an attraction for each other. But, you protest, it would be awkward to cut off a relationship with your children's best friends. What would you tell your kids? I don't know, but it will be a whole lot easier than telling them you are having sex with their best friend's mother!

But among you there must not be even a hint of sexual immorality, or of any kind of impurity, or of greed, because these are improper for God's holy people. —Ephesians 5:3

The covenant nature of marriage calls us to be exclusive. I believe that is why God is so clear about not coveting what you don't have. Why would He care about coveting your neighbor's donkey in Exodus 20? Because when you covet your neighbor's young donkey you are no longer thankful for your donkey and therefore don't treat it as well. When you covet your neighbor's wife, you no longer are thankful for your wife and thus don't love her as well. It is impossible to covet what you don't have and work on what you do have.

> *It is impossible to covet what you don't have and work on what you do have.*

A very mismatched couple, from a human point of view, came in to see us after 6 years of marriage. "Do you think I made a mistake in marrying him?" asked the (very assertive) wife, as her husband cowered on the other end of the couch. In my mind I thought, "You bet you did!" But aloud I simply said, "It's an irrelevant question and one that is not helpful to ponder. You have a covenant relationship with each other and God is able to give you joy in this relationship." To the credit of this wife and her husband, they decided to honor the covenant of marriage, focus on the positives in each other, and find joy in becoming one and being better together.

Could Virginia do better than me for a husband? I am sure she could find someone more intelligent, more disciplined, and more handsome—but that is irrelevant. What great security there is to continue to work on what "God has brought together," rather than tearing our relationship apart by looking around for a "better" partner.

Although our discussion of the priority of marriage over other relationships has focused on opposite-sex relationships, this truth also applies to any friends who become so close that we start sharing ourselves with them in a way that detracts from our spouse being our confidante and friend. Our spouse should never be the one to hear news second-hand. The first call is always to be to them. They are our covenant partner.

A PRIORITY WORTH PROTECTING

Recently we were speaking for a marriage retreat and were housed in a hotel in a part of town that was known for crime. As we entered our hotel room we noticed signs all over the room, including a very prominent sign on the door that said, "Do not leave any valuables in the room. We are not responsible for anything that is taken. Especially do not leave valuables near windows." Well, you can bet every time we left the room I took my computer bag with me and we took our cell phones. Why? Because they were valuable and we wanted to protect them. But I left my toothbrush and even my clothes in the room, thinking, "What thief would want my clothes?" But I took great measures to protect my computer because it was extremely valuable to me.

As we addressed the group on marriage that day, I could not help but share what we had just experienced. We live in a world of "thieves against marriage"; we need to be alert and careful to guard what is so valuable and precious to us.

In Malachi 2 there is a portion of scripture that is best known for the verse in which God says, "I hate divorce."

> But not one has done so who has a remnant of the Spirit. And what did that one do while he was seeking a godly offspring? Take heed then to your spirit, and let no one deal treacherously against the wife of your youth. For I hate divorce," says the Lord, the God of Israel, "and him who covers his garment with wrong," says the Lord of hosts. "So take heed to your spirit, that you do not deal treacherously."
>
> —Malachi 2:15–16 (NASB)

When we hear someone hates something we usually think they are very angry, mean, negative. If, however, you are from a family that has been affected by alcoholism, or you have seen the destruction that alcoholism brings, or have known someone killed by a drunk driver, it would not surprise you to hear a person say, "I hate alcohol." They hate the destructiveness that alcohol brings and that it robs people of experiencing the safety, peace, and true joy in life they deeply long for. In the same way, God states that He hates divorce, not because He is negative, but because He hates that it robs couples, children, and families of experiencing the joy that living out His design for marriage and family affords. God says to "Guard your marriage" not only for the sake of the marriage but also because He wants Godly offspring, and it is much more difficult for children to follow the Lord when they see their Christian parents divorce each other.

Your marriage is more valuable than anything you possess.

Your marriage is more valuable than anything you possess. We guard anything we don't want stolen. We put anti-theft devices on our cars, our homes; we have safes for our valuables—why not be intentional to guard that which is most valuable, relationships?

Occasionally a couple will come in for counseling and ask, "You don't expect us to stay married just for the sake of the children, do you?"

"Why, yes I do," is my reply. What better reason is there? Is your personal happiness so important that you are willing to jeopardize the future and possible eternal life of your children? We as a culture have gone to extreme measures to protect our children: we use car seats, refrain from smoking in their presence, make sure they exercise enough, and so on. Let's also put as much effort into protecting the emotional and spiritual security of the homes our children are raised in.

Why does God hate divorce? Why guard your marriage? Because God does not want you to miss out on all He designed for you in your marriage and family relationships.

*When we put our spouse's needs above our own,
not only will they feel loved,
but it will propel our marriage towards greater intimacy.*

Reminders

☑ Staying in love takes intentionality.

☑ Don't let "little things" eat away at your marriage.

☑ We are called to put our marriage ahead of everything except our relationship with Christ; that includes parents, children, friends, and jobs.

☑ Marriage is not an add-on; it is a paradigm shift.

☑ All decisions now go through the grid: will this strengthen or weaken my marriage?

☑ Our relationships with God and with our spouse are to be exclusive.

☑ Our relationship is of greatest value and should be guarded.

☑ Every affair is intentional.

☑ You cannot work on your marriage while coveting another person.

For Couples

Questions

1. What are some areas in our relationship we maintained more fully earlier in our marriage than we do today?

2. Are there any areas we feel could be strengthened by making our marriage more of a priority?

APPlication

• Plan an overnight away in the next month.

• Be intentional this week in setting time apart for each other in the form of a date night or some other time together.

For Groups

1. Read Matthew 19:1–12. What are some truths Jesus is teaching about marriage in this passage?

2. How long into your marriage did it take you to realize that without a lot of work, your relationship would deteriorate?

3. What do you feel are the "termites" that eat away at most marriages today?

4. What are the things that seem to most easily nudge marriage from being the top priority in your life next to your relationship with Christ?

5. How can you practically keep your relationship with each other a top priority when work and children are constantly vying for number one?

6. What are some things in your home that you value? How do you guard them?

7. What might you do to better guard the greatest treasure you have, your marriage?

Be intentional in pursuing each other

By wisdom a house is built,
  and through understanding it is established;
through knowledge its rooms are filled
  with rare and beautiful treasures.

—Proverbs 24:3–4

*B*efore Virginia and I were married, we couldn't pay close enough attention to each other, ask enough questions, and seek to know everything we could about each other.

BE A STUDENT OF YOUR SPOUSE

Our middle daughter, Lisa, came home one Christmas vacation after dating a young man for only a few weeks. She told us she had invited him over for dinner with some friends. Not sure if their relationship was "established" enough for gifts, she had purchased and wrapped a few things and hidden them in her room in case he brought a gift. Sure enough, he did: among other things, he brought her an onion chopper! "Cut your losses!" I thought, but Lisa had a smile on her face. She went on to explain that she had fixed dinner a few weeks earlier for a ministry leadership group, and he had come into the kitchen to find her chopping onions and crying. She remarked, "I hate cutting onions! They always make me cry." Now that's a good man! He had listened, noted, and responded.

On one of our first dates, I fixed dinner for Virginia. I was a student of her and remembered hearing her say how much she loved avocados. Wanting to show her how much I cared, I bought my first avocado ever and put it in the salad. It was about the texture of a very crisp apple and had no taste . . . but she loved it. Why? Because I had been listening to her, trying to get to know her desires, and then acting on that knowledge.

> You can't please and love your spouse if you do not know your spouse.

She saw my heart, even though the result did not fully meet her desire for a soft and tasty avocado. I wish I could say that for 36 years of marriage I have listened as closely to her desires and been as intentional in trying to show how well I know her and how much I love pleasing her. Although I fail quite often, I am still committed to learning more about my wife even after all these years. This is a joyful process that never ends.

One of my best friends has a card in his wallet with his wife's favorite color, flower, shoe size, dress size, favorite candy, restaurant, etc. He has taken seriously the call to be a student of his wife—and it has paid off.

You can't please and love your spouse if you do not know your spouse. Don't stop asking questions; stay in touch with your changing spouse and what might make him or her feel really loved.

The story is told of a couple returning home after a wonderful 50th anniversary celebration. As was their habit, they shared toast and milk before going to bed. The husband cut off the heel of the loaf of bread and gave it to his wife of 50 years. Perhaps she had toasted one time too often at the party, but for some reason she felt free to speak her mind. "I hate the heel! For 50 years you've given me the heel, but it's my least favorite part of the loaf." The bewildered husband replied, "I love the heel! For 50 years I have been giving you my favorite part of the loaf." I don't know if it is true, but it could be. We too often assume ours spouse's likes and dislikes are the same as ours, and we miss knowing them because we simply stop asking and being a student of their preferences.

One of our friends gave his wife a Hickory Farms sausage log each Christmas in her stocking. After about six years of marriage, his wife asked him if he had ever noticed who ate the sausage log each year.

"Hadn't thought about it," he said, "but I guess it would be me."

"Correct," she said. "I don't like sausage logs!"

Virginia and I recently spoke on this same subject, and a wife shared how her husband of 15 years had spent days baking a choc-olate cake for her birthday. "I *hate* cake!" she shouted. How often we have good intentions in marriage but miss the mark because we do not know our spouse well. How often we hurt our spouse when we do know them but ignore their desires. And how easy it is to hurt our spouse because we fail to see their heart when they miss the mark in their own actions of attempted love for us.

After 37 years of marriage, one of the most stinging (and for-tunately rare) comments Virginia can make to me is, "Don't you even know me?" If I am going to love her well, I need to know her well.

How well do you know each other? Take this 10-question quiz and see. Write your answer in the "Mine" column and what you think your spouse will say in the "My Spouse" column.

Score 5 points for each correct answer (100 total points pos-sible). We have used some popular song titles to rate how you are doing:

	MINE	MY SPOUSE
Favorite TV show		
Favorite color		
Favorite restaurant		
Dream vacation location		
Favorite music singer/band		
Most important ingredient in a weekend away together		
Person you would like to be like		
If you were given $50,000, how would you spend it?		
Best friend (other than your spouse)		
Biggest prayer concern		

SCORING	
90–100 points:	*I've Got You, Babe*
75–85 points:	*Love, Love Me Do*
60–70 points:	*Got To Get You Into My Life*
55 or lower:	*Help!*

EXPRESS LOVE IN THE OTHER'S "LANGUAGE"

Another area in which knowing our spouse is critical is what Gary Chapman has so clearly written about in his book *The Five Love Languages*.[15] His premise is that we all give and receive love primarily in one of five ways: Quality Time, Acts of Service, Gifts, Physical Touch, and Words of Affirmation. Many times we express love to our spouse in ways we would like to receive it. Virginia's parents, though happily married, illustrate how this fact can challenge a marriage. On a given Saturday, Dad would get up early to start a load of wash, then do the dishes after breakfast, do some ironing, vacuum, change the beds, do some yard work, etc. As they fell into bed at night, Mom would say something like "Frank, do you love me?"

He would respond, "Do I love you? I have done the dishes, vacuumed, done the wash, ironed, made the beds, and done yard work, and you want to know if I love you?"

"But you never spent any time with me. We never took a walk, and you never sat on the couch with me!"

Dad was working his tail off, "loving" Mom, while she was getting more and more angry and feeling unloved. Observing this, we explained to them the concept of love languages. Dad's love language was acts of service, so he was trying to show his wife his love by serving her. But Mom's love language was quality time, so she was feeling unloved despite his efforts.

We need to be a student of our spouse and love them in a way they can receive it. When we love them using only our love language, it is as though we were speaking a foreign language to them. You might say all sorts of wonderful things, but if your spouse does not "speak your language," they will not understand your love for them.

We spoke to a couples group on "Love Languages," and one wife shared that her love language was gifts and that for her 30th birthday, her husband really hadn't done anything for her. When she asked him if he had remembered her birthday, he reached in his pocket and said, "Oh, yeah, Happy Birthday," and gave her an envelope with money in it. She shared how hurt she felt, since gifts were her number one love language.

The week after the study she emailed us that her husband had returned from a business trip with a very nice purse and flowers. "The study worked!" she gushed. He had listened and loved her in a way she could receive.

Another email I received clearly shows how important it is to give good information to one's spouse:

"Bob bought me a present yesterday that made my day. He had bought me a cross necklace when our son was born, which I have worn almost daily since. About 6 months ago, I either lost it or it was stolen. I have been sad about it ever since, but have tried not to make a big deal about it. Recently, Bob and I talked about our love languages. I had given him bad information a few years ago, thinking that 'gifts' was a lame love language. [There is no "lame" love language.] I didn't want to make him have to spend money to 'love' me. Anyway, in our conversation, I told him my love language actually is gifts. So, to make a long story short, he came home from a business trip yesterday with a brand new cross necklace for me. He paid for it with money that he had been saving for himself and wrote the most lovely card with it about serving me, our marriage, and our family. It was amazing. I am beaming today!"

ACT ON YOUR KNOWLEDGE

When Jesus washed the disciples' feet, He demonstrated what they were to do and then said,

> *"Now that you know these things, you will be blessed if you do them."* —*John 13:17*

The blessing did not come from knowing cognitively what to do; it came from doing it. Once we know our spouse, the even more critical question is: what are we going to do with that knowledge? To know what is important to our spouse and not respond to it is more hurtful than to not know it.

Both men and women are often guilty of not acting on the knowledge they have, but it seems husbands most often are characterized as "not getting it."

I love the story of another couple that had been married for 50 years. They had had a horrible marriage. For their 50th

128

anniversary, their four children decided to pool their money and send them to a psychiatrist for four sessions. The therapist they saw was a young man who was totally taken aback by their non-stop bickering and yelling for 50 minutes straight. Finally, not knowing what to do, the young therapist got up and spontaneously planted a passionate kiss on the woman's lips. She sat down, stunned. The young therapist pointed to her husband and said, "This is what your wife needs at least three times a week." "Well," said the old man, "I can bring her in on Monday and Wednesday, but on Friday I play golf." Sometimes we just don't get it.

The Apostle Paul wrote to the Romans about God's wrath toward those who "knew God" but did not honor Him or give Him thanks. He says that those people are "without excuse."

The wrath of God is being revealed from heaven against all the godlessness and wickedness of men who suppress the truth by their wickedness, since what may be known about God is plain to them, because God has made it plain to them. For since the creation of the world God's invisible qualities—his eternal power and divine nature—have been clearly seen, being understood from what has been made, so that men are without excuse.

For although they knew God, they neither glorified him as God nor gave thanks to him, but their thinking became futile and their foolish hearts were darkened. Although they claimed to be wise, they became fools and exchanged the glory of the immortal God for images made to look like mortal man and birds and animals and reptiles. —Romans 1:18–23

By knowing God but not responding to Him, they missed out on all God had in store for them; "their thinking became futile," and they exchanged what could have been for what was fake, an imitation. Oh, how often we do that today! We exchange what could have been for an illusion, an imitation—and miss out on the blessing God wishes for us.

Often, in spite of our knowledge, we act as if our spouse should like the same things we do. Virginia and I have friends who are very different from each other. The husband is very spontaneous and loves surprises and adventure. His wife is very structured and is always planning ahead; she does not like surprises and prefers known activities over "adventures." This story took place on Catalina Island on the wife's birthday. The husband picked her up from the school where she taught and whisked her right past their house toward the harbor.

"Why aren't we going home?" she asked, confused.

"*Surprise!*" he said, "I am taking you to the mainland for the weekend for your birthday!"

Instead of the delight he had hoped for he was greeted with dismay. "Who will watch the children?" she asked.

"Already taken care of," he responded.

"I'll need to pack."

"No problem," he said, "I did it for you."

Now she was *really* uneasy, thinking he probably only packed negligees. "But I have things I had planned to get done at the house this weekend. I really don't have time to be gone."

"Well, relax! We are *going!*" was his response, and they did, and they had a terrible weekend. Though he knew his wife, he thought what *he* wanted would be what she *really* wanted. But we are blessed—happy—when we know our *spouse's* desires and, in a spirit of sacrificial service, do for them what they most desire. In this case, knowing his spouse and doing something loving would have been telling her ahead of time that he had a birthday surprise for her in two weeks—he would take care of getting childcare and all the planning, and all she needed to do was clear the weekend and pack.

Recently a couple came to see us, and as the husband walked down the hall, he said, "Boy, did I blow it. I really blew it this week." At least he took ownership of his stuff, which is rare. It was

Mother's Day weekend and, as was his custom, he worked overnight Saturday night. His wife called him at work and reminded him to meet her and the kids at church for Mother's Day at 11 am—it was a special Sunday and family pictures were being taken. He said he was working on the computer, trying to get a couple more days added to their vacation. She said, "Please work on that later. I really want us all to go to church together." The next communication was at 5 pm, when he walked into the

> *When we know what would make our spouse feel loved but don't do it, the message sent is, "I really don't care what you want—it's not that important to me."*

house with a card and some slippers for "the mom." Needless to say, he didn't see her naked that night! When we know what would make our spouse feel loved but don't do it, the message sent is, "I really don't care what you want—it's not that important to me."

We were speakers at a week-long camp and spoke on expressing love by knowing your spouse and putting his or her interests ahead of your own. On the last day of camp, a husband of 15 years shared with us about his love for coffee from a certain coffee shop. His wife did not share his love for this coffee, but had a fondness for coffee from a chain store that he passed each morning as he went to get his cup of coffee. He told us that after hearing our talk, he thought about the fact that for many years he had passed his wife's favorite coffee shop, gotten his coffee from his own favorite place, and never thought to bring her any. So that morning he got up, stopped at *her* coffee shop, bought her favorite coffee, and returned home to waken her with his gift. He told us that as he presented her with the coffee, tears of gladness ran down her cheeks. Often we do not realize that our spouse is not waiting for a big vacation or luxury gift; they simply want to be known and served.

There are many ways that we are able to convey our love to our spouse through the discipline of action. Perhaps our wife loves flowers, but we feel it a waste of money. Might the occasional expense of flowers speak a loud "I love you"? It can be a simple thing, such as remembering her favorite coffee and bringing it to her. Maybe it is putting on a favorite negligee and surprising him in bed, or perhaps it is putting the lid to the toilet down or emptying the trash. Maybe it is having dinner ready when he arrives home from work. The specifics of the list are really not that important, but the fact that your spouse knows you are thinking about them and wanting to put their desires ahead of yours will speak volumes.

When we put our spouse's needs above our own,
not only will they feel loved,
but it will propel our marriage towards greater intimacy.

Reminders

☑ When a couple is courting, it is easy to pay attention to each other.

☑ After being married for awhile, we tend to become a less attentive student of our spouse.

☑ Being aware of our spouse's "Love Language" plays a critical role in knowing how best to love them.

☑ Love is not only knowing our spouse, but specifically acting on that knowledge.

☑ It is often the "little" things done for our spouse that foster love.

For Couples

Questions

1. Try to identify and rank each other's love languages.

2. Ask each other how you could better love each other in the other's own "language."

APPlication

• Do something for your spouse this week that you did during your first year of marriage that you know would mean a lot to him or her.

• Intentionally show love to your spouse this week in his or her preferred "love language."

For Groups

1. Share with the group your love language and how this concept has affected your marriage.

2. Read 1 Corinthians 12:7–26 and share how this passage can apply to marriages.

3. What is it that contributes to our giving "the heel of the loaf of bread" to our spouse and never knowing they dislike it?

4. Why do you think it is so easy, the longer we are married, to become lazy in being students of our spouse and not act on that knowledge?

5. Share about a time your spouse "nailed it" by knowing you and acting on that knowledge in a positive way.

7

Give each other love and respect

*However, each one of you also must love his
wife as he loves himself, and the wife must
respect her husband.* —Ephesians 5:33

Virginia and I were having a group of couples at our house for dinner the night before we were to give a talk at a Couples' Night Out on the subject of "What husbands and wives wish the other knew about them." To jump start our conversation around the dinner table, we asked our guests how they would answer the question. The men went first, and the consensus was "The number one thing we would like our wives to know is that being respected by them is the greatest gift they can give us. Second, we like sex. That's about it—if we have respect and sex, we are pretty content."

The ladies went next. Their list was a bit longer, and sex was not in the top two. Their number one item, however, was that being cherished by their husbands was their greatest desire.

The men wanted to be respected, and the women wanted to be cherished. Over our years of marriage counseling, the areas of respect and love have been central indicators of the health of a marriage.

When counseling, we will often ask the wife (on a scale of 1–10, 10 being high), how cherished she feels by her husband. We will then ask the husband, using the same scale, how respected he feels. I will never forget the man who stared at us and then asked, "Is zero the lowest I can go?"

So what is it that puts in the heart of a man the deep desire to be respected by his wife and in the heart of a wife the yearning to be cherished by her husband—and why does it seem so difficult for so many couples?

THE RESULT OF A SINFUL CHOICE

We believe the clue came way back in Genesis, after Adam and Eve ate the forbidden fruit and sin entered the world. In Genesis 3:16–19 the results of the fall are explained, gender specifically, to Adam and Eve. While God is addressing Eve, He says,

> *"Your desire will be for your husband, and he will rule over you."* —Genesis 3:16b

It is important to understand the meaning of the word "desire" as used here. There are at least three interpretations that I know of.

1. Perhaps it means that, as a result of the fall, women will want a sexual relationship with their husband, but their husband will rule over them. I have counseled men for over 30 years and have yet to hear a man say, "Sex, sex, sex, that's all she wants! Could you just ask her to back off?" This is clearly not what God is saying to Eve.

2. Many people believe it means that, as a result of the fall, women will have a desire for relational intimacy in their marriage, but their husbands will rule over them. It is true that God wants us to have a close relationship with our spouse, but that is not what is being talked about here. In the next chapter of Genesis, this same phrase is used:

"If you do what is right, will you not be accepted? But if you do not do what is right, sin is crouching at your door; it desires to have you, but you must master it."

—*Genesis 4:7*

Sin and Satan have no desire for a close relationship with you. All they want to do is to control you. Therefore, if you take this back to Genesis 3:16, you come to the third interpretation:

3. Because of the fall, women's tendency will be to attempt to control their husbands, and their husbands will attempt to rule over them. This interpretation makes sense. Many husbands complain to me that their wives are always correcting them, telling them how they should or could have done better. These husbands question why their children ever ask them anything, because inevitably, their wives overrule their decisions. They say they often feel like a child and that their wife is the mom. Many wives try to control their husbands, not physically, but verbally, by nagging and complaining and trying to change their husbands.

Many husbands, on the other hand, instead of protecting and caring for their wives, have ruled over them and neglected their own role as providers and protectors. Rather than serving sacrificially with Christ-like characteristics, husbands often try to force their wives to serve them through a variety of methods. Sadly, it is often through rage, anger, and intimidation—the very antithesis of Christ-like leadership.

It is critical to understand that what God is talking about in these verses, addressed to both husband and wife, is associated with the curse that resulted from sin. In no way is any of this a blessing. "He will rule over you" is a blessing neither to the woman nor to the man. It is not how God desires us to be.

We know this to be true because the other major portion of scripture directed specifically to men and to women is found in the Apostle Paul's letter to the Ephesians:

Wives, submit to your husbands as to the Lord. For the husband is the head of the wife as Christ is the head of the church, his body, of which he is the Savior. Now as the church submits to Christ, so also wives should submit to their husbands in everything.

Husbands, love your wives, just as Christ loved the church and gave himself up for her to make her holy, cleansing her by the washing with water through the word, and to present her to himself as a radiant church, without stain or wrinkle or any other blemish, but holy and blameless. In this same way, husbands ought to love their wives as their own bodies. He who loves his wife loves himself. After all, no one ever hated his own body, but he feeds and cares for it, just as Christ does the church—for we are members of his body. "For this reason a man will leave his father and mother and be united to his wife, and the two will become one flesh." This is a profound mystery—but I am talking about Christ and the church. However, each one of you also must love his wife as he loves himself, and the wife must respect her husband.

—*Ephesians 5:22–33*

ANTIDOTE TO THE FALL

In the passage above, the Apostle Paul, led by the Holy Spirit, gives the antidote to the fall:

- Husbands, because of the fall, your tendency is to rule over your wives, either through domination or passivity. Love them by serving them.
- Wives, because of the fall, your tendency is to control your husbands. Love them by respecting and submitting to them.

Paul does not say, "Now, y'all love and respect each other." He specifically tells husbands to love and lead, and wives to submit and respect.

These commands are independent and unconditional. Scripture does not say, "Husbands, love your wife *if* your wife is nice" or "*unless* your wife is mean to you." Nor does scripture say, "Wives, submit to and respect your husbands *if* he agrees with you" or "*unless* he doesn't treat you the way you imagined he would." When husbands lovingly lead their wives and wives respect and submit to their husbands, they have the greatest possibility of getting back to what God designed marriage to be in Eden.

Let's consider the specific roles and responsibilities of husbands and wives in carrying out these commands. The passage starts by saying that the husband is the authority in the home:

> *For the husband is the head of the wife as Christ is the head of the church . . .*   *—Ephesians 5:23a*

This means that the husband has been given responsibility for his wife. It is impossible to be given responsibility for something without being given authority as well. Note that although Eve sinned first and ate the forbidden fruit, Adam is identified as the one responsible for sin entering the world:

> *Therefore, just as sin entered the world through one man . . .*   *—Romans 5:12a*

I believe Adam is held responsible because God has appointed husbands to be the providers and protectors of their families.

Many a man simply hears "For the husband is the head of the wife" and then closes the Bible and says, "That's enough Bible for today." He then goes on to think that if he is the head of the wife, then he is a "boss," and everyone should be there to serve him. Not nearly! Read the next clause: "For the husband is the head of the wife *as Christ is the head of the church.*" Christ certainly has authority over the church. No one ever is confused, thinking the Church has authority over Christ; nor should one think the wife has authority over her husband. *But*, before you protest, remember that Christ *never used his authority for his selfish ends.* Christ always used his authority to do whatever was best for his bride, the Church.

It is critical here to acknowledge that this position of authority and primary responsibility in the home is positional. That means it is assigned by God, not "earned" because one is smarter, stronger, or earns more money. In the economy of God, He chose to make the husband responsible for the family. In the Trinity, God the Son is submissive to God the Father. All three members of the Trinity have equality, but they have different roles in the relationship. Both husband and wife are to partner together, but the husband is the one to whom God has given ultimate responsibility and authority. In our family, what this means practically is that I am responsible for leading our family. The best decision I ever made was to marry someone smarter and more gifted than I. This does not mean that Virginia is now the head of our home; it just means I was really, really smart to marry up, and that we are able to be better *together*, as we value each other's input and work as a team.

HUSBANDS ARE CALLED TO DO FOUR THINGS:

1. Be the chief servant.

Husbands, love your wives, just as Christ loved the church and gave himself up for her . . . —Ephesians 5:25

Christ was the chief servant and used His authority to serve.

"For even the Son of Man did not come to be served, but to serve, and to give his life as a ransom for many." —Mark 10:45

Both husbands and wives are to serve each other, but the husband is to use his authority to serve his wife and family. For too long, men have seen their wives as the ones to serve them rather than regarding themselves as the chief servant. Certainly both husband and wife are called to serve, but ultimately it is the husband who is called to be the chief servant, because he has been appointed to this position and has been given the authority to carry it out. Christ Himself is the husband's example to follow: Christ, who came not to be served, but to serve.

> *Ultimately it is the husband who is called to be the chief servant.*

Very practically, let's say the family is eating a chicken dinner. In many families, the food is put in front of the husband as the head of the family, and he takes the best piece of meat and passes the rest on to the other members of the family. In the Christian family, I would suggest that the father, because he is the head of the family and has authority, takes the platter and passes it to his wife, she takes some and passes it to their children, and he gets what is left, because he has authority to serve his family first.

Or it may be that he watches a "chick flick" with his wife and daughters rather than Monday night football. (Okay, well, maybe he suggests watching the "chick flick" on *Tuesday* night instead of another show he would prefer.) A Christ-following husband should always look for ways to use his authority to serve his wife.

2. Be a servant leader.

Jesus took initiative with the church and led the church. Too many men become "Whatever you wish, dear" men and never lead, or are missing altogether from the home. Leadership certainly does not mean dictatorship, but it does mean leading. Often this simply means taking initiative. We are called to lead actively, but as servants, not as selfish tyrants.

I once heard a guest speaker from Egypt say he had learned the two most important words for a man to know in the English language: "Yes, dear." The comment received a good laugh, but should have evoked tears. As I travel and speak at men's conferences, I observe a lot of men in their 60s, 70s, and 80s who have become "Yes, dear" men. They are nice and kind, and do whatever their wife wishes, but they are void of life. Their wives are frustrated with a husband who neither leads nor takes initiative. These couples may lead peaceful lives with little conflict, husband and wife each living their own lives—but their relationship is void of passion, intimacy, vibrancy, and life.

> *Whoever wants to become great among you must be your servant.*

Somewhere along the line, the husband quit being a servant leader and his wife stepped into the void, and both are missing out on what could have been a dynamic partnership.

> *Jesus called them together and said, "You know that those who are regarded as rulers of the Gentiles lord it over them, and their high officials exercise authority over them. Not so with you. Instead, whoever wants to become great among you must be your servant..."* —Mark 10:42–43

3. Take spiritual initiative.

Jesus cleansed the Church by the washing with water through the Word. We as husbands are called to be spiritual leaders in our home. That certainly does not mean we need to know more or be more educated, but what it does mean is that we take the initiative in our home to lead our family spiritually. It could start with making sure we give thanks before each meal, making sure we are all in church on Sunday, and reading the Bible in our homes. Our wives should not be pulling the family along spiritually.

4. Help her become more radiant.

Jesus interacted with the Church, to present her to himself as a radiant church, without stain or wrinkle or any other blemish, but holy and blameless. I am not sure about all that this means, but I know that part of my role as a husband is to help my wife become more and more radiant.

When I officiate at a wedding, I often look to the groom and say, "Look at your bride and see how radiant she is! Thirty years from now, she should look *more* radiant."

One of the ways I do this for Virginia is by knowing her dreams and desires, her gifts and abilities, so that I can help her become all she can be. It may mean staying home with the children so she can take a class or go to a study or just relax. Too often, our wives are worn out because they have taken care of us instead of us taking care of them.

WIVES ARE CALLED TO DO TWO THINGS:

1. Submit to your husbands.

It is very important that we understand submission does not mean a lack of equality. Remember, our example is the relationship of the Trinity. In Jesus we find the model both for the husband and the wife. The husband is to love his wife as Christ loves the Church; the wife is to submit to her husband as Christ submits to God the Father. Ephesians 5 also gives the example of the church submitting to Christ. The most vivid account is in the Garden of Gethsemane, when Jesus reasons with the Father and asks if there might be another way to accomplish the salvation of the world—yet He submits to the Father's plan.

*He withdrew about a stone's throw beyond them, knelt down
and prayed, "Father, if you are willing, take this cup from me;
yet not my will, but yours be done."* —Luke 22:41–42

Jesus' submission to the Father in no way made Him less than
the Father. Jesus' obedience to the will of the Father also did not
make Him less than the Father.

*"I have brought you glory on earth by completing the work you
gave me to do."* —John 17:4

So in the marriage relationship, submission does not mean
a lack of full interaction and contribution from the wife. It does
mean that after full interaction is given, unless the husband is
asking the wife to do something specifically forbidden in scripture, she is to submit to her husband's decision.

Given the tendency for wives to try to control their husbands as
a result of the fall, we like the definition of submission that Larry
Crabb gives.

"Submission is resisting the urge to control."[16]

In her rich book, *The True Woman*, Susan Hunt sums up the
heart behind submission:

I cannot give logical arguments for submission. It defies
logic that Jesus would release all the glories of heaven so
He could give *us* the glory of heaven. Submission is not
about logic; it is about love.

Jesus loved us so much that He voluntarily submitted
to death on a cross. His command is that wives are to
submit to their husbands. It is a gift that we voluntarily
give to the man we have vowed to love in obedience to
the Savior we love. . . .

God said that man needs a helper. The true woman
celebrates this calling and becomes affirming rather

than adversarial, compassionate rather than controlling, a partner rather than a protagonist. She becomes substantively rather than superficially submissive.

The true woman is not afraid to place herself in a position of submission. She does not have to grasp; she does not have to control. Her fear dissolves in the light of God's covenant promise to be her God and to live within her. Submission is simply a demonstration of her confidence in the sovereign power of the Lord God. Submission is a reflection of her redemption.[17]

2. Respect your husband.

Even though we often talk more about submission, perhaps respect is the more difficult one to fully understand. When a woman tries to control her husband or overrule his decisions, he tends to feel disrespected. Often a woman feels she is trying to "improve" her husband, but he is feeling disrespected.

When Virginia and I are driving together, sometimes she will take it upon herself to "help me drive better." A wife might say things like "Watch out for that pothole! Don't you think you should slow down?" or "Be careful—our exit is coming up in a mile. Don't you think you should start changing lanes?" Instead of feeling helped, the man "hears" in her questions the implication "You don't know what you are doing."

Cynthia Heald puts it well:

> Some ways I tended to show disrespect for him were to challenge his decisions and, more often than not, to offer my alternatives to those decisions. I would interrupt and correct him in front of others, especially in front of the children. In my effort to inspire him to be his very best, I would give him my lecture entitled, "Whatever you do, it's just not good enough." He could be home more, he could spend more time with the children, he

could read more, he could be more sensitive, he could be more spiritual.

One day it dawned on me that I was not Jack's personal Holy Spirit. My job was to respect him and to fulfill *my* God-given role in our marriage. I was not given to Jack to redo him, but to complement him. When I finally became aware of the log in my eye, I was able to back off and begin to give him time and encouragement to lead. He, then, slowly but confidently became the head of our home.

I have learned that as I respect Jack, I am not so inclined to manipulate him. My respect for Jack was necessary to free him to be the husband and father he was meant to be.[18]

Respect is often simply expressing your "need" of your husband, your appreciation for him, and then allowing him to serve without correction from you, even if he doesn't "get it all right."

It is important to note that loving your wife and respecting and submitting to your husband are both commands. Therefore, they cannot be simply responses to emotions, but are decisions of the will.

IF WE DON'T FIX IT, CHAOS REIGNS

When men are not respected, they often withdraw and/or respond in anger and rage. When men do not lead lovingly, the wives often take over and relational chaos reigns.

I received an email from a medical doctor asking for advice regarding a couple he sees:

The wife called because the husband's anger has been escalating. From his perspective, his wife is controlling to the extreme. He has tried to deal with his frustration, but feels she is not willing to make changes. He now stays away from home as much as he can or tries to avoid talking to her when he is at home.

This pattern of control and withdrawal, though not always as dramatic as the story above, is repeated in countless homes every day. The solution to this chaos, however, is not separation and divorce—it is love and respect.

WE DON'T HAVE A CLUE

A major part of the problem in the area of showing love and respect to each other is that as a man, I don't think like Virginia, and she doesn't think like me. I know exactly how I want her to respect me, but she doesn't have a clue. She knows how she wants me to cherish her, but I don't have a clue. Both of us tend to show love to each other the way we want to receive it. We also have a tendency to think, "My spouse should just know this is important to me." Neither of us appear to be very good at mind reading.

We need to give each other the freedom to say, "When you say that, I feel very disrespected" or "I would feel more cherished and loved if you . . ."

I met with the man mentioned in the referral from the doctor above. After identifying that, on a scale of 1–10, his wife was likely a 2 in how much she felt cherished by her husband, I challenged him to do something this week to show his love for his wife. I asked him, "What could you do that would help her feel cherished? What are some things she likes that you could bring her or do for her?" His face twisted, and he groaned and finally said, "Wow, that's a really tough one. I really don't know what she would like." I suggested then that perhaps his first assignment was to find out what would make her feel loved so he could do it.

THE ROAD BACK

No matter what point you are in your marriage, you can take the road back to what God wishes for you.

For men

Men, apologize to your wife for not having taken the initiative as you ought and not having served your wife as a Christ-like husband should. Promise her that you will take more initiative and attempt to put her interests ahead of your own and cherish her as she should be cherished as your wife.

Let me be very practical here: taking initiative means taking initiative, not having all the answers. For instance: when you come home and observe it's been a tough day and dinner isn't started, don't say, "Where's dinner? What have you been doing all day?" Say something like, "Looks like it's been a tough day here. Why don't we go out to dinner at that new Italian place?" Your wife may respond, "That sounds great, but we had Italian last week. Could we have Mexican tonight? I hear there is a great new place in town." You say, "Great, let's go." You have taken initiative but not dictated. That is servant leadership.

Many of us as men are clueless about what to do. I remember a man in his 70s coming in to my office. He said his wife told him he was selfish and never cared about her. He went on to describe to me his routine when he arrived home. He walked in the door, asked what was for dinner, went up to his room, changed his clothes, came back down, got the newspaper, and turned on the news, and waited until his wife told him dinner was ready.

I suggested that perhaps his wife would feel more cared for if when he came in the door, he were to walk over to her, give her a hug, and ask how her day was and whether there were anything he could do to help her.

He looked at me in astonishment and said, "I have never thought of that. Do you think it would help?"

"Yes, I do."

Before he left he said, "Would you mind writing down the things I am supposed to ask her before I change my clothes, so I can put them on my dashboard and practice before I get out of the car?"

For women

Ladies, let him lead. Many men try to lead, only to find their wives telling them they did it wrong. And remember, when a man fails at home, he quits. Thank him for his efforts and don't criticize him for his lack of perfect execution. Find ways to affirm him and thank him for what he does. He needs to be needed, just as you need to be cherished.

An affirmed man will be much more likely to be vulnerable and engage with you. Let's say you are having dinner guests and you are working together to get ready. You discover that your tablecloth is dirty and needs to be laundered. You are busy cooking, so you ask your husband if he will run to the store and get some laundry detergent. He says, "Sure," and runs out the door, forgetting his cell phone. He gets to the store and sees the 96 possibilities of laundry detergent before him. He has heard that Tide is good, so he grabs Tide and heads home. He walks in the door and you say, "Tide?? You got Tide?! Don't you know anything? Have you never done the wash? We get the generic brand to save money!" Your loving husband responds, "Fine, you get it next time! I am sick and tired of you never appreciating me!" and you bicker and fight until the company arrives, and then you are both nice for the next three hours and then go back to bickering after they leave.

Here is the same situation, take two: The husband walks in the door with Tide, and the wife says, "Thanks so much for doing that—it was a big help to me." He says, "Oh, I was afraid I had gotten the wrong kind." His wife says, "Actually, you did. We usually buy the generic brand, but thanks so much for your help." Do you see the difference? Ladies, if you will just refrain from commenting for a few seconds, we husbands will admit we might have gotten it wrong. We assume we are usually wrong. But when you attack us, we get defensive and withdraw, and both of us lose.

Do you remember the "avocado story" in chapter 6? As the years go on, it's easy for a husband to stop listening to his wife's "likes" and no longer try to "get the avocado." Even worse, some husbands see the avocado as a needless expense to the meal, or say to themselves, "I don't like it, so I'm not going to purchase it."

It is also easy for wives to be critical of the hard avocado and not express appreciation that her husband is at least trying. When husbands are continually criticized for "missing" on the execution of the expression of their heart, they decide not to try again. Very few of us repeatedly try that which we keep failing at.

BENEFIT OF RESPONDING TO GOD'S DIRECTIONS TO CHERISH AND RESPECT

Husbands loving their wives and wives respecting their husbands are actions first, not emotions. You cannot command an emotion. We are to look for ways to cherish and to show respect. As we do this, our relationship with our spouse will spiral up rather than down.

Husbands who are respected are more likely to become all God designed them to be, just as wives who are cherished by their husbands are more likely to become all God designed them to be.

Husbands who are respected tend to cherish their wives more fully, just as wives who are cherished tend to show respect to their husbands more fully.

When we put our spouse's needs above our own,
not only will they feel loved,
but it will propel our marriage towards greater intimacy.

Reminders

☑ Respect from a wife is one of the greatest gifts a woman can give her husband.

☑ Cherishing his wife is one of the greatest gifts a man can give his wife.

☑ As a result of the fall, women will have a tendency to try to control their husbands.

☑ As a result of the fall, men will have a tendency to try to rule over their wives or abdicate their leadership role.

☑ Scripture instructs men to:
   Serve their wives
   Lovingly lead their wives
   Engage with their wives spiritually
   Help their wives become more radiant

☑ Scripture instructs wives to:
   Submit to their husbands
   Show respect to their husbands

☑ Men don't naturally know how to cherish their wives.

☑ Wives don't naturally know how to respect their husbands.

☑ A cherished wife becomes more the wife God designed her to be.

☑ A respected husband becomes more the husband God designed him to be.

For Couples

Questions

1. Men, finish this sentence: "I feel most respected by you when . . ."

2. Wives, finish this sentence: "I feel most cherished by you when . . ."

APPlication

- Men: Surprise your wife this week by doing something for or with her that you know would mean a lot to her, but you would normally not do.

- Women: This week, focus on affirming your husband and refraining from correcting him or instructing him on how he could have "done it better."

For Groups

1. How did you see or do you still see respect or lack of respect being shown to your father?

2. How did you see or do you still see your father cherishing or not cherishing your mother?

3. Do you agree with the author's remarks regarding Genesis 3:16?

4. How have you seen the instructions to men to love their wives serve as an antidote to the curse?

5. Why do you think there is so much resistance to the idea of submission in our culture?

6. Read Ephesians 5:22–33.

   • How do you think the principles of this passage should be lived out in marriages in this time, in this culture?

   • Describe a couple you know that you feel most fully demonstrates the principles the Apostle Paul sets forth in this passage.

8

Experience the joy in sacrificial love

*"Greater love has no one than this, that he lay
down his life for his friends."* —*John 15:13*

*I*n the first chapter, we introduced the concept of sacrificial love. Let's look at it a bit more closely here, because everything we are saying ultimately hangs on our understanding of what love really is.

The fullest expression of love is always associated with sacrifice. Unfortunately, when we hear the word "sacrifice," we usually associate it with something that costs us but has no return. Although we are not to act lovingly merely for the "return" we might receive, the truth is that usually when we express sacrificial love to another, usually it positively affects how that person responds to us.

We really can't talk about how we are to love each other without looking at the perfect expression of love found in Christ and expressed in scripture. This is not simply a "Sunday School" answer; it is Truth. If we define "love" in our own terms, we get into all sorts of trouble. What one person defines as love may be abuse to another. Trusting our own feelings or heart to define love is risky at best.

> *"The heart is deceitful above all things*
> *and beyond cure.*
> *Who can understand it?"*   *—Jeremiah 17:9*

This is why the Apostle Paul in Ephesians 5:25 tells husbands to love their wives *as Christ loved the church.* Christ is the definition of love. Husbands are to love their wives as Christ loved the church, not as they feel like in the moment or as their hormones suggest.

If we as husbands have not read scripture to see how Christ loved the church, we will have no basis on which to know how to love and serve our wives. If wives have not read scripture to see how Jesus Himself interacted with God the Father, they will have no way of fully understanding their worth and what submission means.

THE MODEL OF SACRIFICIAL LOVE

Perhaps one of the reasons we have difficulty grasping the sacrificial love of God for us is that we really honestly have no concept of what a great sacrifice it was for Christ to leave heaven, live on earth, be crucified, and be separated from the Father for the first time in eternity.

Sacrifice has always been connected with love:

> *"For God so loved the world that He gave his one and only*
> *Son..."*   *—John 3:16a*

God sacrificed His very best—His only Son—as an expression of love for us. Love is most fully expressed through sacrifice. Certainly we see the ultimate expression of this in Christ demonstrating His love for us by coming to earth, living among us, and being crucified for us.

> *"Greater love has no one than this, that he lay down his life for*
> *his friends."*   *—John 15:13*

Our youngest daughter was recently married and moved indefinitely to Uganda, Africa. When we tell people her story, they often say something like, "She must really have a deep love for the children to sacrifice so much to move there." We also have a nephew who is an avid surfer. He went to be a "missionary" in Australia among the surfers. No one has said, "He must have a deep love for the surfers in Australia to move there." The reality is that our nephew and our daughter both have sincere hearts to be used by God to minister to those in need. But my point is that we associate "true love" with what we deem to be sacrificial actions.

> *Sacrifice has always been connected with love.*

1 Corinthians 13, the great love chapter, states clearly that love "does not insist on its own way."

The reality is that many of us simply are not *willing* to put the needs of our spouse ahead of our own. The story is told of a man who was quite ill and went with his wife to see the doctor. After a lengthy office visit with the man, the doctor asked if he could speak with the wife, alone. The doctor told her that her husband was very ill. He said to her, "If you want your husband to live, you need to do the following. When he gets up in the morning, get him his newspaper and coffee. Fix him his favorite breakfast and send him off to work with affection. When he returns home, greet him with a kiss and let him unwind by watching the news while you fix his favorite meal for dinner. Don't bother him with the issues of your day, and don't ask endless questions about his. After dinner, let him watch sports or whatever he wants on TV. When he comes to bed, satisfy his every sexual desire. If you do this, he will live; if you don't, he will die."

When the wife came out, her husband said, "Dear, what did the doctor say?"

"You're going to die!"

As funny as this is, it is often not far from the truth. We know what our spouse needs to fully come alive, but are often not willing to do it.

About 20 years ago, we were in the same room when Lou told Grace, his wife of 30 years, that he had never loved her. It was a bit awkward to be there in that moment. From a human standpoint, they should never have gotten married. Lou was a rough and tough cowboy, was raised in multiple orphanages, was a heavy equipment mechanic, and loved rodeos and drag racing. Grace was a lovely, refined Dutch woman, with never a hair out of place. She enjoyed craft shows, quilt exhibits, and tea parties. After this conversation that we were privy to, Lou and Grace separated for about a year and a half. They eventually came back together to try to make their marriage work.

Love is a decision of the will before it is a feeling of the heart.

Not too long after they had gotten back together, we attended the *Nutcracker* ballet with them. At intermission I said to Lou, "So, you love ballet?" He looked me straight in the eyes and said, "I love my wife." And that was the right answer. He hated ballet. He probably felt somewhat like our youngest daughter did when we asked her how she liked the ballet: "Oh, it was okay, except for the dancing." Grace now goes to rodeos and drag races, and Lou goes to craft shows and ballets—not all the time, but if one says, "It would mean a lot to me if you would go with me," the other is in.

Today we would put Lou and Grace on our short list of happily married couples. They have recently celebrated their 50th wedding anniversary. They have 3 children, 7 grandchildren, and 3 great-grandchildren. They both have told us numerous times, "We are so glad we stayed together and didn't give up!"

Contrast Lou and Grace with another couple that came to see us in which the wife also enjoyed ballet and the theater. She told us of her love of ballet and how much it would mean to her if her husband would go with her occasionally. He rolled his eyes and minced no words explaining that he had no desire to attend, but had offered to pay for two season tickets to the ballet. His wife was free to invite any female friend she wished to the ballet and dinner. He would even send a driver, since she didn't want to drive to the city. With tears running down her face she said, "He doesn't get it. I want him to experience the ballet with me." He chose not to, and missed an opportunity to show true love for his wife.

The discipline of sacrificial love means putting the needs and desires of your spouse ahead of your own. As it has been said, "Love is a choice." It is a decision of the will before it is a feeling of the heart.

When a husband tells me, "I have fallen out of love with my wife," I try to gently correct him by pointing out to him that a more accurate statement would be, "I have chosen not to love my wife."

Last year Virginia and I sat with a couple that came in at the husband's request. He explained, during the counseling session, that he didn't know if he could go on much longer in the marriage because his wife didn't show love to him. As we explored the issues with them more fully, he added, "If she loved me, she would make love with me every other day to meet my sexual needs, and she wouldn't refuse to do what I want her to do with me sexually."

A few days later we received a copy of an e-mail that a friend of ours, whose wife has struggled with mental illness and acute depression, had sent to a man who was similarly struggling in his marriage with a wife who also had severe depression. Below is a short excerpt from the email.

> And what God has called together, He doesn't want broken. I would be lying if I said that the word divorce never entered my mind, but it never really did enter my thinking. Vows are vows. In the dark nights sometimes our thoughts go to the idea that we might be better off if only we could flee the marriage. But in the morning, standing and staying is of God, and by staying you have honored God in ways perhaps more noble and glorious than any of the Christian leaders you might deeply admire. Honoring your vow is a deep thing that God has asked of you and placed upon you, and by honoring it, you in your own small way have been helping God's kingdom come to life here on earth, because a vow has been kept in a world that treats vows like tissue paper: easily shredded and torn. Kept vows build God's shalom like very little else does.
>
> There is an old story of an older missionary couple that came back to the States on a steamship after a long and faithful career of serving God overseas, invisibly and without much reward. They were at the rail of the ship as it came to its berth, and there was much fanfare and commotion there on the dock to greet a famous dignitary who was coming home. He mumbled something to his wife about how they weren't getting any kind of a welcoming or recognition. His wife paused a moment and then said, "But, honey, we're not home yet."
>
> One day you will look Jesus in the eye, and He will know what you have done, and He will look in your eyes and whisper, "well done." Not perfectly done: Lord knows how imperfectly I've handled this calling He has put upon

me, and the things I am ashamed of, and the failures that I know and carry. But one day, you'll be home, and all things will be made right. One day. So keep hoping. This world is not all there is. This world is upside down. But, one day, your wife will be fully alive, and so will you. One day. So keep hoping. As you live in the messiness of the present, keep hoping for the wonder of the future. It is beyond what you can imagine. So keep hoping.

Wow. One man was ready to leave his wife because she wouldn't do whatever, whenever he wanted sexually, while the other man has stayed faithful to a wife who seldom, if ever, can do whatever, whenever.

Which husband truly loved his wife? When we get married to have "our" needs met, we set ourselves up for all sorts of disappointments when our spouse doesn't deliver or when life's twists and turns make it impossible for our spouse to please us as they may have done early on in our marriage.

When we get married to serve our spouse, we will never run out of opportunities to do that, regardless of what life throws our way.

I love to tell the story of Steve and Marla. Marla was a ministry assistant at a church in which I served as the director of Family Ministries. I had heard that Steve and Marla had gotten divorced and then later married each other again. Because of my area of responsibility at the church, I was especially interested in hearing their story. I asked Marla to confirm what I had heard about them, and she said it was true.

"What was it that caused you to fall in love with each other again before you remarried?" I asked.

"Oh, we didn't 'fall in love' again."

"Oh, I'm sorry—I thought you remarried."

"We did," she said.

"What changed your feelings for each other?"

"They didn't," she responded.

I felt we were going in circles until she finally explained, "We didn't marry again because we felt like it; we married out of obedience because we had no grounds for divorce. Now we have feelings for each other, but those followed our decision to remarry."

For many of us, our practice of sacrificial love towards our spouse will not be as dramatic as reuniting after a divorce or staying faithful for 35 years to a wife who often cannot respond to you. For many of us, an act of sacrificial love will be going shopping with our spouse, or watching sports together, or having more sex, or having less sex, or having more conversations.

Sometimes it is as simple as doing something our spouse really feels strongly about, even when we have no interest. It could mean recycling even when we believe all the recyclables end up together in a landfill somewhere, just because our spouse feels strongly about ecology. It could mean listening to country music because your spouse believes it is music. It could mean having a dog because your spouse loves pets.

When we were first married, I would shove the shower curtain against the wall after taking a shower. Virginia said I should pull it back closed. This did not make sense to me. I shared my thinking, explaining that the next day when I need to take a shower, the curtain would be open already, so I could walk in and *then* close it. She said, "Oh, no, if you don't pull it closed, it will mildew." It was really important to her, so now I always pull the curtain closed. Each time I pull it closed, I am saying in a small way, "I love you, Virginia."

After we had spoken on sacrificial love to a church on the Pacific Coast, the pastor got up in front of his congregation and said, "I guess I'll be walking on the beach." He then went on to explain that when he and his wife had received the call to come to this coastal church, his wife was ecstatic because she loved walking on the beach. Her husband told her, "I am happy for us to have a home close to the beach, but you need to know up front that I won't be walking the beach with you. I hate walking on the beach." Had his love for the beach changed? No, just his expression of his love for his wife.

> *True love is first an act of obedience rather than a response to an emotional or hormonal feeling.*

Lest you feel that marriage consists primarily of "gut it out, even when you are miserable," read on. But don't miss the point that true love is first an act of obedience rather than a response to an emotional or hormonal feeling.

I don't know what sacrificial love will look like in your marriage, but I do know that as you seek to make your marriage a priority, learn to know each other, and look for ways to sacrificially love each other, you will experience a new level of intimacy with each other.

THE DISCIPLINE OF SACRIFICIAL LOVE WITHOUT RECIPROCATION

We live in such an I-will-if-you-will culture: "I will respect my husband when he starts loving me." Or, "I will start loving my wife when she starts showing respect to me."

When husbands love their wives as Christ calls them to, wives will generally respond in positive ways. When wives submit to their husbands and show respect to them, their husbands will generally respond in a positive manner.

Our actions, however, are not to be based on our spouse's reaction to us, but based on our relationship to Christ. Again, love of our spouse is first and foremost an act of obedience.

Very rarely will anyone die for a righteous man, though for a good man someone might possibly dare to die. But God demonstrates his own love for us in this: While we were still sinners, Christ died for us.　　　　　　　　　*—Romans 5:7–8*

A couple came into our office and the man immediately started out our session by saying, "Tell my wife she needs to follow scripture. Tell her to obey scripture by submitting to me and not depriving me sexually." After a pause, Virginia turned to him and asked, "Do you know any other passages of scripture, such as 'Husbands, love your wives, just as Christ loved the church.' ?"

The feelings of love will ebb and flow over time, but the commandment to love is constant.

A few years ago, Virginia was speaking to a gathering of women on submission. At the end of the talk, a woman stated her belief that wives were supposed to submit to their husbands as long as the husbands were doing what the wife felt was the right thing to do. There are no conditions given in scripture, however, except "as to the Lord." Wives are to submit to their husbands unless they are asked to do something sinful. Husbands are to love their wives regardless, no exceptions.

The directions to husbands and wives are gender specific and individual. Husbands are not told to "make" their wives submit and wives are not told to "make" their husbands love them:

Wives, submit to your husbands as to the Lord. [Period. No further conditions.] . . . *Husbands, love your wives, just as Christ loved the church and gave himself up for her* [No conditions.]　　　　　　　　　*—Ephesians 5:22, 25*

Perhaps one of the problems with staying married is the way we become married. We generally become married to someone because we "feel" so much in love with them. When we no longer "feel" in love with them, we assume we have married the wrong person. The feelings of love will ebb and flow over time, but the commandment to love is constant. We are *commanded* to love—and that means love must be more than feelings, since we are not able to command feelings. When they were younger and under our care, I was able to command our daughters to do the dishes after dinner, but I was not able to command them to be happy while doing them.

In his wonderful book *The Meaning of Marriage*, Tim Keller writes,

> So if your definition of "love" stresses affectionate feelings more than unselfish actions, you will cripple your ability to maintain and grow strong love relationships. On the other hand, if you stress the action of love over the feeling, you enhance and establish the feeling. That is one of the secrets of living life, as well as of marriage.[19]

As we will explore more fully later, God certainly does not wish us to be miserable in our marriages. He is able to help us love our spouse and bring about new health to our marriage.

We started the book with a story about Wendy and John and how she wished she'd made him more Jell-O. At some point in life, each of us will look back and reflect on our marriage and what could have made it more what we desired and what God designed it to be.

When you look back, what do you think you will say? Perhaps: "I wish I'd gone shopping more with her." Or, "I wish I'd not been so tight with my money," or "I wish I'd sat with him in the hot tub more." . . . Why wait? Why not go shopping with her now? Why not splurge on that vacation together? Why not hop in the hot tub now and reap the benefits of loving each other more fully today?

I was once the officiant at a wedding that was held in a cemetery. Before you think of this as morbid, imagine the beautiful large trees, fields of green grass, and the quietness of those in the neighborhood. The wedding itself was held in an incredibly beautiful rock chapel. Knowing I was performing a wedding in a cemetery, I couldn't pass up making a comment on this during the service: "It is unexpectedly appropriate that you are being married in a cemetery, because actually, until you die to yourself, you will never truly live for each other." Perhaps all weddings should be done in cemeteries.

I would be remiss to finish this chapter without acknowledging that in order for sacrificial love to bring about intimacy in marriage, your spouse must receive that love and respond to it. Some of the individuals I admire the most are those who have loved well even when their spouse did not respond to them with love or intimacy. Despite the efforts of the spouse who wished the marriage to continue, some of these have ended in divorce because one spouse refused to be loved and to respond with love.

One of my best friends loved well and sacrificed well, and yet his wife made the decision to leave him for another. Since his completeness and wholeness was in Christ and not in his spouse, he was devastated but not destroyed. He continued to love and serve the Lord, even in the midst of much emotional pain.

I am reminded that Jesus Himself, the definition of sacrificial love and the perfect lover of mankind, was rejected by many who would not receive His love. John 1 tells us that Jesus came to many but only those who responded were able to realize the gift of life He had for them.

He came to that which was his own, but his own did not receive him. Yet to all who did receive him, to those who believed in his name, he gave the right to become children of God.

—John 1:11–12

Perhaps those who have sacrificially loved yet been rejected by their spouse may understand more fully than most of us a bit of what the perfect sacrificial lover must have felt when His love was not received. Jesus understands—and He will not desert you.

When we put our spouse's needs above our own,

not only will they feel loved,

but it will propel our marriage towards greater intimacy.

Reminders

☑ Love is most fully shown through sacrifice.

☑ God demonstrated love perfectly for us with the sacrifice of His only Son.

☑ If God had created us the same, I couldn't show love to Virginia because I would just be doing what I selfishly want.

☑ Love is first doing the right thing before "feeling" the right thing.

☑ We are to love sacrificially even when those we love don't respond as we wish.

☑ There are times when a spouse truly loves sacrificially but the other spouse will not receive the love and walks away. Jesus understands and will meet us in such times.

☑ Dying to oneself is the prerequisite of living for another.

For Couples

Questions

1. What are the times you feel most sacrificially loved by your spouse?

2. What are some ways you would feel more sacrificially loved by your spouse?

APPlication

♦ Before you leave the house, ask each other if there is something you could do for your spouse that would make their day go more easily—and then do it if at all possible.

♦ Shock your spouse this week by doing something he/she could not "repay" you for.

For Groups

1. What are some of the "lame" definitions of love in our culture today in relationship to marriage?

2. What would you say to your dating daughter if she asked you to help her know how to judge if her boyfriend really loves her?

3. Read Philippians 2:1–11. What are some truths from this passage that, if applied, could revolutionize marriages?

4. Why is an understanding of Christ's sacrificial love so important if we are to love one another well?

5. How can we encourage couples toward the action of love when they don't have the feeling of love for their spouse?

6. What are some ways you have been the recipient of sacrificial love?

7. Why would we feel better about ourselves when we act sacrificially toward our spouse even if they don't seem to respond sacrificially to us?

8. What do you think most couples will regret as they look back on their marriages?

9. Pray with each other that you will love your spouse more sacrificially this week.

Find new life through forgiveness

Be kind and compassionate to one another,
forgiving each other, just as in Christ God
forgave you.   —Ephesians 4:32

bout this time, you may be feeling like a good friend of ours who went to one of these exclusive health clinics for corporate executives in which, over a 24-hour period, they run every test known to man and give you a complete report on your condition and health risks, as well as a prescription for the course of action you need to take if you want to experience a long and healthy life.

At the end of the day, the report came back: "Lose 80 pounds or prepare for a heart attack within the next 5 years." Our friend's age was finally catching up with his junior-high lifestyle. He had a choice to make: listen to the advice of the experts, or continue living as he had, ignoring the signs of compromised health he was experiencing.

MARITAL CHECK-UP

As you have read the preceding chapters, you may feel that you, too, have had a "check-up" that has revealed areas in your life and the life of your spouse in which you are doing really well—and perhaps revealed other areas that need change.

Your response to this knowledge can make the difference between having a compromised or dying marriage and having a vital, joyful marriage. We have found, in our own marriage as well as in countless others, that the longer we are married, the easier it is not to take care of our marriage as we ought. As the years pass, we have a choice: to deal with the issues

> *We are never more Christ-like than when we forgive.*

that have challenged our marriage, or to ignore them and continue to live a compromised marriage.

It is so easy in our fast-paced world to keep on living day to day and not make time to connect with our spouse, rather than to work on our issues and experience more marital health.

I believe many of us don't get "marital check-ups" because we are afraid of what will be discovered. Too many of us are content to live with "poor marital health" rather than to discover and act on what we might need to do. I remember being in a small group Bible study where the topic one particular week was on telling the truth. During the discussion, one participant said, "I would rather live with a compromised marriage than risk telling the truth to my spouse."

When we operate with such fear of conversation and confrontation, it is easy to become distant from each other and start living separate lives. It is easy for resentments and bitterness to build, just as plaque builds up in the arteries. Slowly, and often very subtly, our "marital circulation" is cut off from our heart, and our relationship dies unless surgery occurs.

I love the YouTube clip in which comedian Brian Regan talks about eye exams. He says he went 6 years without having his eyes checked. After he finally saw his eye doctor, he said, "Man, I could have been *seeing* things! How could instantly-improved vision *not* be at the top of your to-do list? 'Oh, I'll see tomorrow. I don't have *time* to see clearly.' "[20]

Too many married couples go years without discussing how well they are "seeing" in their marriage. To paraphrase Brian Regan, "Man, I could have had an improved marriage! How could an improved marriage not be at the top of your to-do list?"

Forgiveness is the procedure that allows us to "see" again, to have "healthy hearts"—to experience a healthy marriage. In the words of Corrie ten Boom:

> Forgiveness is the key which unlocks the door of resentment and the handcuffs of hatred. It breaks the chains of bitterness and the shackles of selfishness. The forgiveness of Jesus not only takes away our sins, it makes them as if they had never been.[21]

THE SACRIFICE THAT BRINGS LIFE

As image bearers of Christ, we are never more Christ-like than when we forgive. The ultimate expression of love from Christ was His sacrificial death on the cross so that we could be reconciled to God.

Forgiveness in marriage is an act of sacrificial love so that we might be reconciled to each other. There is no one thing that destroys relationships and marriages more than lack of forgiveness. It was sin in the Garden of Eden that caused Adam and Eve to cover themselves and live in shame. Sin always separates us from each other. Just as husband and wife are not able to become physically one unless they are naked, so they are not able to become fully one relationally and spiritually while wearing cloaks of shame and bitterness.

175

When we refuse to forgive each other, Satan wins, and we lose. Satan wins because we have, in essence, said Christ's death on the cross was not sufficient to bring reconciliation. This is one of the reasons the divorce of two believing parents is so catastrophic for their children, who think, "God is powerful to raise the dead, but not to preserve my parents' marriage? Why would I want to follow a God like that?"

THREE CONSTRUCTION OPTIONS

When a marriage collapses, one of three things happens:

1. The couple sees the collapse of their marriage, but refuse to do the work of reconstruction. One or both walk away, believing it is better and easier to build elsewhere than to repair their marriage.
2. They try to ignore the collapse and just rebuild on the rubble, believing that appearance counts more than substance.
3. They do the work of removing the rubble and start building a stronger relationship on the new, solid foundation.

Let's look at these three options and see how they play out in marriages today.

Option One: Walk Away

This option leaves a wake of debris in the rear view mirror. It does not examine what caused the collapse, but moves into another "building," assuming it will be stronger than the first. It seldom is:

> Past statistics have shown that in the U.S. 50% percent of first marriages, 67% of second, and 73% of third marriages end in divorce.[22]

This first option is the "easiest" of the three and the one most often recommended by others. "Cut your losses and move on." It may seem easiest at the moment, but you still "own the rubble" and will have to deal with it in the future in one way or another.

Often there is blaming and resentment towards each other. Neither spouse is willing to take the time and hard work to address the issues, so they live with bitterness, resentment, and a refusal to forgive.

Sadly, one spouse may wish to rebuild, but the other walks away. It is often fueled by the "immediate gratification" syndrome that believes that "If it makes me happy to walk away because it is easier, it will always be easier. If it is easier, it will make me happy, and if I am happy, everyone else will be happy as well." As flawed as this logic is, it brings immediate relief and thus is readily pursued.

The spouse that is the victim of unrepentant infidelity, desertion, or abuse may also choose to walk away. As tragic as this is, for the protection of that spouse and/or the children, this option is often the lesser of two evils.

In either case, however, forgiveness is critical to the health of all involved. There may never be reconciliation, because that requires confession and repentance, but forgiveness does not require a response from the offending spouse. Forgiveness is unilateral. Forgiveness is leaving your bitterness and vengeance at the foot of the cross and letting God take care of the justice part.

Forgiveness turns the person over to the Lord to deal with and allows the forgiver to live in freedom as one who is Christ-like by offering forgiveness. In the words of the great theologian Richard Nixon: "Always remember, others may hate you, but those who hate you don't win unless you hate them—and then you destroy yourself."[23]

In the words of the Apostle Paul:

Do not take revenge, my friends, but leave room for God's wrath, for it is written: "It is mine to avenge; I will repay," says the Lord. —Romans 12:19

It is very important, however, to realize that forgiveness does not mean enabling the continuance of sinful behavior. It is possible to forgive your spouse but not return to them. You may forgive a spouse for gambling away your savings, but this does not mean you need to allow him to have independent access to your funds.

Option Two: Ignore the Collapse

Option two is when couples say, "Let's just move on, start anew, and forget what has happened in the past." It sounds great, but in actuality, it is like building right on top of the rubble. To the onlooker, everything appears fine, until there is even the smallest tremor, which rocks the marriage. Because there is no solid foundation, the next collapse occurs easily, simply "burying" the first collapse—making the cause of the original collapse extremely difficult to deal with.

Moving on in this way may look like forgiveness, but is really an attempt at "forgetfulness." It is often a very attractive position for the offending spouse. They use phrases such as, "Let's just move on from today. I don't want to involve you in any more pain." What they often mean is, "I don't want to take responsibility for my sinful action."

William and Jane had been married 12 years when William was sexually unfaithful to Jane. He refused counseling, but finally and grudgingly agreed to stop sleeping with his mistress and move on with his wife and family. They never really dealt with the sin, just picked their marriage back up, acting as though nothing had happened. To the outside world, nothing had. They were respected in their community and church. Their marriage "house" looked spectacular from the outside. Then one day, the ground began to shake and the beautiful house collapsed into shambles: he was having another affair. It really was no surprise. The first affair had never been dealt with, so their marriage never had a solid foundation on which to be built.

With no true repentance, there couldn't be true reconciliation, and therefore their oneness in marriage had never been re-established. We don't talk much about repentance today because it strikes at the heart of our pride. One cannot repent without having a humble and contrite heart. The definition of repentance is to turn 180 degrees and go the opposite direction. In practical terms, the litmus test of repentance is: has it changed the heart and actions of the one repenting?

The Apostle Paul confirms this definition when he says:

Repent, then, and turn to God, so that your sins may be wiped out, that times of refreshing may come from the Lord . . .
—*Acts 3:19*

Later, when addressing King Agrippa, Paul states:

". . . I preached that they should repent and turn to God and prove their repentance by their deeds."   —*Acts 26:20b*

Paul affirms three things about repentance: one, it involves a turning from sinful behavior; two, it manifests itself in new actions; three, it allows you to be renewed and refreshed in the Lord.

Option Three: Clear the Rubble and Rebuild

Option three requires a lot of work. The fact of the collapse must be recognized (acknowledgment). The reason for the collapse must be admitted (confession). A pledge must be made that the decisions which led to the collapse will not be repeated (repentance). And finally, there must be willingness on the part of the couple to work together to rebuild (forgiveness). When acknowledgment, confession, repentance, and forgiveness take place, couples are able to start rebuilding on a solid foundation.

Jay and Pam had been married for 10 years when Jay had an affair. Their marriage was difficult, what with all the traveling in Pam's job, the stress of Jay's job, their financial struggles, and infertility to top it all off. When Jay's affair became known, Jay and Pam went to three different counselors who said, "Take option one. You have no children; cut your losses and move on." When they came to our office, we asked them why they had made an appointment. "We want to make our marriage work." "Great," we said, "then let's roll up our sleeves and get to work, because there is a lot of rubble to move." Part of removing the rubble for them included moving away from their community to avoid further contact with the mistress, selling their house and moving in with his folks to reduce their financial stress, her quitting her job—and a great deal of tears, confession, and forgiveness.

> *The question we need to ask is, "Do I really want our marriage to get well?"*

Today, 14 years later, God is using this couple to bring healing to many marriages and to bear witness to the incredible riches of forgiveness made possible through the cross and a willingness to meet at the cross and extend and receive forgiveness. Oh, yes: the daughter born to them in their "infertility" was a blessing beyond all they ever hoped or imagined.

DEALING WITH "LESSER" SINS

For many of us there has never been adultery, abuse, or such, but we have hurt each other and sinned against each other, and because of failure to own our sin, confess it, repent of it, and experience forgiveness, our relationships are significantly damaged as well.

The question we need to ask is, "Do I really want our marriage to get well?" Too many hurt spouses continue to harbor bitterness, saying things like "After what you did to me, I will never forgive you!" or "I want you to know how it feels to be hurt so deeply before I forgive you."

Many of us, if we are honest, would agree with Sigmund Freud when he said (quoting the poet Heinrich Heine), "Yes, one must forgive one's enemies—but not before they have been hanged."[24]

Most of us might be willing to embrace the forgiveness concept, but not before our spouse has "paid." Isn't that the feeling you get when you read about Peter asking Jesus how many times he needs to forgive his brother in Matthew 19? It appears that his heart is not really asking "How long am I to forgive?" but rather "How long until I don't need to forgive?"

The forgiveness that brings reconciliation is not just refusing to retaliate, or even ignoring what happened. Forgiveness that brings healing occurs when our hearts are changed to the point we actually want the best for the person who has hurt us. This is what the Apostle Paul is saying when he instructs us:

> *Bless those who persecute you; bless and do not curse.*
> —*Romans 12:14*

Lewis B. Smedes puts it this way:

> You will know that forgiveness has begun when you recall those who hurt you and feel the power to wish them well.[25]

One of the exercises Virginia and I ask couples to do on their road to healing is to each make a list of all the ways they have sinned against their mate. At an appointed time they read their lists to each other, without justification or excuses. They then offer forgiveness to each other as part of the clearing away of the rubble. The second part of the exercise is for each to say to their spouse, "I have asked forgiveness for the ways I know I have sinned against you or hurt you. Are there some areas that I missed that you want to make me aware of, so we can clear that rubble as well?"

A woman wrote to me after she and her husband had worked through this forgiveness exercise. "The amount of 'calm honesty' is so easy for us after confessing and forgiving each other. It is really amazing."

PREPARING TO FORGIVE

Some people are just nice. They look at the positive side of things. Our daughter Lisa is like that. When she was four years old, she came home one day from playing with some neighbor children with a knot on her head.

"Lisa, what happened to your head?!" we asked.

"Oh, my friend hit me with a hammer when we were playing."

"That's horrible!" we exclaimed.

"Well, at least he didn't have a nail."

Today Lisa responds to difficult situations in a similar fashion because that is how she lives life. In the same way, we can "prepare" to be good forgivers by cultivating a heart of forgiveness and not hard hearts. Gail MacDonald said it well:

> I am convinced that we do not learn to forgive in the hour of crisis; we actually train for it. Is it strange to say that in our best moments we prepare for the potential worst ones? In this case, we study the meanings of forgiveness and how it is portrayed in Scripture. We watch and learn from others who are going through situations needing forgiveness. And we monitor our own spirits to observe our progress in times of small irritation or conflict. Are we instantly vindictive or easily drawn to give grace?[26]

Whether we are "nice" naturally or really have to work on it, we are all called to forgive, even when our emotions or disposition do not lean that way. Forgiveness is an action of the will first before it is an emotion of the heart. We are the beneficiaries of Christ's obedience to death, and He is the one we are to imitate.

Be kind and compassionate to one another, forgiving each other, just as in Christ God forgave you. —*Ephesians 4:32*

FREEDOM THROUGH FORGIVENESS

Whether you have been devastated by infidelity, hurt by neglect, distressed by disrespect, or injured by an indifferent spouse, forgiveness is necessary for your marriage to thrive.

Gerald Sittser, in his very helpful book *A Grace Disguised,* speaks about the freedom Christ made provision for on the cross.

> However difficult, forgiveness in the end brings freedom to the one who gives it. Forgiving people let God run the universe. They let God punish wrongdoers as He wills, and they let God show mercy as He wills, too. That is what Job and Joseph came to . . . That is also what Jesus decided, as demonstrated by the pardon He granted His accusers and executioners while dying on the cross. . . .
>
> Forgiving people want God's mercy to win out. They want the world to be healed of its pain and delivered from the evil that threatens at every turn to destroy it utterly, including the evil that threatens to destroy their own souls.[27]

MEET ME AT THE CROSS

We were at a conference this past year in which Wayne Cordeiro, founding pastor of New Hope Church in Honolulu, Hawaii, was one of the speakers. He told the story of the importance of always having a meeting place for your family if you ever get separated or wander off the path. In our family it would be like telling the girls, before we went into Disneyland, that if for any reason we get separated, go to the ticket counter for the Matterhorn. This was reassuring to all of us and critical information to remember in case we were separated.

Wayne said that when he and his wife got married, they agreed on what he called a "Christian Pre-Nuptial Agreement." It went like this: they pledged to each other that if for any reason during their marriage one of them were to wander off or become separated from the other, the person who had not wandered off would wait for the lost spouse at the foot of the cross. I loved that. When we wait at the foot of the cross, we can't help but remember that no matter what our spouse has done, if he or she returns to the cross, we are on level ground. When I stand at the foot of the cross, I am reminded of my sin and my need of forgiveness. When I stand at the foot of the cross, it reminds me that whatever my spouse has done to injure me pales in comparison to what I did to put my Savior on the cross. It reminds me that because of Christ's forgiveness of my sins, I have a relationship with God, and because of His death and resurrection, He desires me to have a relationship through forgiveness with my spouse.

At the cross we are made "as if we have never sinned." When we are "as if we have never sinned," we are back in Eden. When we are back in Eden, we are "naked and without shame" and now able to experience more intimacy in every aspect of our lives.

Do you see why forgiveness is so critical, yet difficult? Satan *hates* forgiveness, because at the cross Satan is defeated and God wins. At the cross we are able to be reunited with God and with our spouse in the way God originally designed it to be.

"Please remember, if we get separated, to meet me at the cross."

*When we put our spouse's needs above our own,
not only will they feel loved,
but it will propel our marriage towards greater intimacy.*

Reminders

☑ Just as physical check-ups alert us to areas where change is needed, so marital check-ups should also alert us to areas where change is needed to further our marital health.

☑ Sometimes we live with compromised health because we are afraid of what may be required of us if we let our lives be more fully examined.

☑ Forgiveness is often needed to restore us to the marital health that we have desired and God designed us to experience.

☑ When we forgive, we are most Christ-like.

☑ Rebuilding our marriages requires the hard work of removing the "rubble" of poor choices in order to rebuild on a solid foundation.

☑ As difficult as forgiveness is, it always brings freedom.

☑ Being committed to "meeting at the cross" is critical for marital reconciliation and life.

For Couples

Questions

1. Which of the three options for dealing with marital distress do you feel you are most prone to?

2. As you look over your married life, where has forgiveness been most difficult? Where has it been used to bring restoration of relationship?

APPlication

• Each of you take some time to write down the areas in which you feel you have hurt your spouse and need to ask forgiveness.

• After you have each written your lists, share them with each other, with no comment other than "thank you."

• Next, ask each other if there are any ways you have hurt your spouse that you did not think of. After they share those areas, ask forgiveness for those as well.

For Groups

1. How was conflict handled in your family of origin?

2. Can you identify patterns in which your parents used option one, two, or three to deal with sin and distress?

3. What are areas in which you think couples are most prone to say, "I could never forgive my spouse for . . ."

4. How can one forgive a spouse without enabling continued sinful behavior?

5. Read Matthew 18:19–35.

   • What does Peter seem to be asking Jesus?

   • What does this passage highlight regarding what we need to do ourselves before being able to forgive another?

   • How does this story address what happens to those who refuse to forgive?

6. Share a story about yourself or someone you know where forgiveness brought a new sense of freedom and intimacy.

Delight in each other

"Whoever finds his life will lose it, and whoever loses his life for my sake will find it."   —*Matthew 10:39*

*T*his *is* the irony. When we put the desires and needs of our spouse ahead of our own, we actually are much more likely to have our desires and needs met as well.

DELIGHT IN THE IRONY OF COUNTERINTUITIVE BEHAVIOR

God did not set this whole thing up so we would be holy but miserable. In the end, we win, too. Since we were created in the image of God, it makes sense that we are most fully alive when we imitate Christ. It is a bit odd that we are often duped into believing that real life comes when we follow the one that only came to "steal and kill and destroy" instead of the One who came "that we might have life to the full."

But serving must not be done to manipulate others. We don't serve our spouse so they *owe* us one. We serve because it is what God calls us to. I'll never forget speaking to a men's group and challenging them to love their wives as Christ loved the church. I told them that one of the practical applications of this is that the husband, as head of the home, is to be the chief servant as he imitates Christ, because Christ came to serve, not to be served. I suggested they go home and make a commitment to look for ways to serve their wives and put the interests of their wives ahead of their own. I also remarked that as a wife is cared for, she often starts responding more to her husband with respect, appreciation, and even sexual responsiveness. A few days later I happened to see a man who had been at the seminar. "It doesn't work," he complained. "I've served my wife for three days, and it makes no difference." I told him this was not a three-day experiment but a lifetime assignment.

For most wives, it takes a bit longer than three days for her to believe there has been a genuine change in her husband. I'm reminded of the story of a husband and wife who lacked affection in their relationship. Mrs. Richards, after noticing her neighbor bringing home flowers for his wife five nights in a row and passionately embracing her each time, said to her husband, "You know, I've observed the strangest thing. Every evening this week our neighbor has walked to his door with a gift and a bouquet of flowers, gave them to his wife, and kissed her. Isn't that romantic? Why can't you do that?"

Mr. Richards replied, "I couldn't do that—I hardly know her!"

But as time passed, Mr. Richards began to think that such treatment must be what really excites women. So he went out and bought a big box of candy and a bouquet of his wife's favorite flowers. Arriving home a little early that afternoon, he rang the doorbell, and when his wife appeared, he passionately embraced her. To his surprise, she collapsed on the floor in a heap of despair.

"My gosh," he exclaimed, "what happened?"

She wailed, "This has been the worst day! Our son received a terrible report card, Mom was admitted to the hospital, the roast burned, the washing machine broke, and now, to top it all off, you come home drunk!"

It is sad that when we do something really nice for each other, acting in a biblical manner, our spouse assumes we are drunk or want something in return.

It is not always the husband who is impatient. We have met with many couples where the wife has said something to the effect, "I have really tried to be respectful this week. I think I've done a good job, but if he doesn't start to change soon, I'm afraid I will have to take over again."

> *When wives respect their husbands and husbands cherish their wives, you won't want a new spouse—you'll have one.*

But we have seen it again and again: when wives respect their husbands and husbands cherish their wives, you won't want a new spouse—you'll have one.

MODELS OF DELIGHT

Most of us have very few role models of those who have put their spouse ahead of themselves and found true delight in marriage and each other as God originally designed. For Virginia and me, one such couple is Bill and JoAnn Shore. Bill and JoAnn were our hosts while we were speaking at a marriage conference at their church recently.

Bill is 81 and JoAnn is 79. This is a couple that *delights* in each other. On the Sunday we were staying with them, Virginia and I left the house around 7:30 am in order to arrive in time for the early service. After church, we mentioned to them our concern that we may have wakened them when we left. Bill said, "Oh, we were awake at 7 but stayed in bed and . . . well, I guess you know." They are a delightful couple and delight in each other. At every meal we ate together, Bill would give JoAnn a kiss just after the prayer for the meal. I noticed that every time he walked past her in the house he would pinch her bottom or give it a loving smack.

Bill and JoAnn have been married 59 years. When we asked them what would they have done differently if they had it to do over again, they both answered, "Come to Christ at an earlier age." You don't have to hang around Bill and JoAnn long to see that their relationship with Christ is most important to them. At 81 and 79 they are hosting dinners and Bible Studies, and discipling men and women. One teacher at the church was pointed out to us as being one of the 5th generation of those Bill has discipled who are, in turn, now discipling others.

As soon as Bill and JoAnn came to Christ, they decided to put Him first and their marriage second. They have been serving Him, each other, their children, and the kingdom ever since. They are not in Florida collecting seashells; they are in Pennsylvania serving others and finding delight in it and each other.

God's plan is perfect—ironic, but perfect. When we put Him and others ahead of ourselves, *we* are the ones who experience the delight.

You might say, "Nice story, but Philadelphia is a bit far to go to see a good model of marriage." I bet you could find one in your own church. Here are some practical directions for finding a couple to model for you or to mentor you in your marriage.

1. Choose a couple you respect that is a bit farther along in marriage than you and your spouse.

2. Don't tell them you want them to mentor you. That will scare most couples off, because they may see a mentor as someone who has a curriculum or specific plan to use in mentoring. Just ask them if they would go out to lunch with you, your treat. This is way cheaper than therapy and likely as effective.

3. Watch them over time and make sure they seem to be living lives that reflect a deep love for the Lord and for each other, both as individuals and as a couple.
4. Make sure they love God's word and are involved in church.
5. Do they seem real? Are they open about their joys and struggles?
6. Do they seem to like you, and do you like them?
7. Will they meet with you regularly?
8. If so, you have a mentor couple!

SACRIFICIAL LOVE BRINGS DELIGHT IN COMMUNICATION

Scripture instructs us:

Do not let any unwholesome talk come out of your mouths, but only what is helpful for building others up according to their needs, that it may benefit those who listen.

—Ephesians 4:29

In our take-care-of-me system, we usually say what will make us feel better. But according to Ephesians 4:29, when we are acting Christ-like we are aware of our spouse's needs and say the things that will benefit our spouse—"those who listen" rather than us. Modern psychology says, "Get it off your chest so you will feel better and benefit." Scripture says to get off your chest only those things that will benefit, not you, but your spouse.

This does not mean you are not able to correct or to offer advice. If, in fact, we love each other and want the best for each other, we will point out areas that will help our spouse be more the man or woman God desires them to be.

As we say so often in our office to couples that are constantly blaming each other and in essence saying, "If only he/she would change": it really is about the heart. When you know your spouse is *for* you, it's significantly easier to accept your spouse's suggestions, criticism, and critique. But when your hearts are not for each other, you will likely bristle at any suggestion.

When Tom Brady, one of the greatest NFL quarterbacks of all time, was a teenager, he was coached and mentored by Tom Martinez. Even after three Superbowl victories and a Hall of Fame career, Brady would ask Martinez to critique him after every game. Instead of resenting Martinez' remarks, he welcomed them, because he knew Martinez was *for* him and only wanted him to improve.[28]

> *Love always does what is best and most pleasing for our spouse.*

Virginia and I find that how we take critique from each other is a barometer of our marriage. When we are doing well and I am feeling respected by Virginia, she can critique me and I welcome it. When we are not doing well, however, she could tell me something as simple as, "You have a booger in your nose," and I would snap, "Why do you have to be so negative?"

When we start being more aware of our spouse's communication style and try to cater to that rather than acting in a way that essentially says, "This is who I am, so get used to it!" then *we* will benefit as well.

Husbands, when you start answering the question "How was your day?" with more than a grunt or "Fine" and actually expound a bit on the day, I think you will find your wife coming alive a bit more. When you take the initiative and inquire about how your wife's day has been, and ask if you could help her with dinner or the kids, you will likely start seeing a responsive wife in ways you have not seen before.

Wives, when you are willing to accept a "Cliffs Notes" response to your "How did your day go?" question, to resist the urge to start an interrogation about his day, and to stop following each statement he makes with a question that comes across to him as "Why did you do that?", I think you will start seeing a husband who will open up a bit more and start connecting more.

Once while counseling a married couple, the wife talked constantly throughout the session. At one point she complained that her husband never asked about her day. Gently I said, "I bet he's afraid you'll never stop talking if he asks."

We both want to connect; we just do it so differently. When we understand and appreciate those differences, we will start delighting in our communication.

SACRIFICIAL LOVE BRINGS DELIGHT IN MARITAL SEXUALITY

When we "do what comes naturally," we can have sex. But when we do what will be most pleasing to our spouse and best for them, we can make love. Love always does what is best and most pleasing for our spouse.

When a husband realizes that foreplay to a woman has much more to do with his conversation and relational connection than with his hands, and if he then seeks to meet his wife's desires before his own, he will be surprised to see her change in attitude toward physical involvement.

When a man does "what comes naturally" and finishes the sexual act in short order, assuming "if I like it, she should like it", he may have had sex, but he didn't make love. Making love is sacrificial and requires putting the desires, interests, and needs of your spouse ahead of yours.

Many men settle for "show up" sex, in which their wife merely "shows up" and says "Okay, I'm here; just go ahead and get it over with." But when a man acts unselfishly in this area, he will often find an involved wife—and that is much more satisfying to a man.

It is interesting to me how the exact same phrase is used twice in Song of Solomon:

> *"His left arm is under my head,*
> *and his right arm embraces me.*
> *Daughters of Jerusalem, I charge you*
> *by the gazelles and by the does of the field:*
> *Do not arouse or awaken love*
> *until it so desires."*
>
> —*Song of Songs 2:6–7; also 8:3–4*

The meaning of "embraces" is literally "to fondle." The author is saying that the husband is lying with his wife with his left hand under her head, likely speaking to her, and his right hand stimulating her sexually in a way she would not experience if he just put his own sexual instincts first. Again, the irony is that when a man takes care of his wife's needs for connection and stimulation first, his experience is far more satisfying than if he just does what would quickly satisfy him.

Likewise, when a wife accepts that her husband's desire for sexual involvement is from the Lord, understands how it ties in so fully to the way he views himself and his self esteem, and takes initiative sexually with him, I think she will be surprised at his increased care for her emotional and sexual needs.

Some very dear friends of ours wrote us the email below, which eloquently describes the scenario in many bedrooms. Ben was a medical student who could come home for only a few hours every few days.

> Sally: "Ben had been doing a particularly demanding rotation where we were seeing him for 2 hours/3 days, leaving very little if any time for us to just talk. We fell into bed one night, exhausted, when he started batting his eyelashes at me. I reminded him of your lesson that women need to

women need to have relationship to have sex while men have sex to be relational, and explained how disconnected I felt due to our lack of time together. Being the wise man and quick learner that he is, we proceeded to have two wonderful hours of heart talk and reconnecting! (Yes! Two whole hours where he was just as engaged in the conversation as I was!) By the end of those two hours of heart talk, I was the one batting my eyelashes at him! After we had sex, I gasped at how late it was, or I should say, early in the morning by now. Ben grinned and said, 'If we had done it my way, we would have been done two hours ago!' He was right, but we fell fast asleep *both* being happy!"

Ben: "Also, just to add my 2 cents' worth to the story that Sally shared: That late evening started off with me being extremely exhausted from work. The last thing on my mind was to listen to anyone. I was just concerned about getting a 'relation' and drifting off to sleep (how barbaric and simplistic, I must say). But then, Sally wanted to share some things, and I distinctly remember asking the Lord, 'Please, Lord, I need your strength to listen. Not that I wanted sex (yeah, right!), but because this is someone precious and she has some heart-felt things she'd like to share.' The first few minutes were a struggle between half-sleep and half-awake. But after we started talking more, we both really delved into the discussion, and it was so meaningful to both of us. I must say that the ensuing intimacy was *so* rich because of the spiritual, emotional, and mental bonding that went on prior to it; and I'm speaking from a male's perspective, too. It's through experiences like this that I realize how very much God cares for us as human beings, and how very well He knows us!"

And that is the irony, is it not? When Ben put Sally's needs above his own, he not only expressed sacrificial love to Sally, but also experienced way more pleasure and satisfaction sexually than he could imagine.

Do you get the drift? The irony *is* an integral part of God's plan. If we were alike, we would not be able to love sacrificially. When we are loved sacrificially, we respond to that love in ways that bring delight to all. Following the Lord does take sacrifice and denying ourselves some of "Satan's pleasures," but the delight of doing so is so worthwhile.

We were designed to be Christ-like, and to the extent that we are, we are able to experience more fully what God always had in store for us. The Apostle Paul expresses it well:

> *However, as it is written:*
> *"No eye has seen,*
> *no ear has heard,*
> *no mind has conceived*
> *what God has prepared for those who love him"*
> *—1 Corinthians 2:9*

SACRIFICIAL LOVE BRINGS DELIGHT IN OUR UNIQUENESS

Virginia and I have an ongoing "discussion" regarding our dishwasher. I believe the reason you buy a dishwasher is so that *dirty* dishes can be washed without any prep work. Virginia likes to rinse the dishes off so they don't mess up the dishwasher and leave scum around the rubber seals. I "heard" her last week, rolled up my sleeves, and cleaned off all the scum, thinking to myself that instead of taking so much time over the years to rinse dishes after every meal, it only took me 15 minutes to scrub the dishwasher, and we are ready to go! Her attention to detail really bugs me at times.

Yesterday, on the other hand, I needed to find some important papers related to our cars. I asked Virginia where the papers were, *and she knew!* I *love* that about her! I really love her attention to detail!

When we see that we are both "fearfully and wonderfully made" by God, we can begin to delight in our uniqueness. We truly are "better together" when we appreciate each other's characteristics and work as marriage partners.

THE DELIGHT OF FINISHING WELL

Our friend Bob Kraning told us that when he was about to marry his wife, Carol, his father pulled him aside, reminded him that there had been 100 years of marriage without a divorce on both his side and Carol's family's side, and simply said, "Don't mess it up." Bob and Carol are finishing well. They have now logged 54 years of marriage; they delight in each other and are what I call a successful couple.

Bob tells the story of flying from Denver to Ontario after speaking at a weekend conference. He was exhausted as he plopped himself down in a row of empty seats. His hope for a row to himself for a couple hours of sleep was dashed when a man dressed in an extremely expensive suit, wearing alligator shoes and carrying a matching attaché case, sat down in his row. The man noticed Bob's Bible on the middle seat and said without hesitation, "Sir, you are sitting next to one of the most successful men you will likely ever meet. I am just returning from a three-week trip to China. I own three businesses in four countries. I have over 1,000 employees and everything money can buy—and I don't believe a word in that book you have there."

Not being one to sit back without responding, Bob said, "Well, isn't that something?! You have likely never sat next to a more successful man than me. I have been married to the same wife for over 25 years. She is my best friend, and I have missed her so much these three days while I have been away. She will be waiting to meet me at the airport. I have two teenage sons who are like friends to me. I love to be at their football games, and they seem to like hanging out with me. Every morning I get up and look forward to a job that allows me to have a positive effect on people's everyday lives and, actually, their eternal destiny—and I believe everything in that book I have here. I guess you would call me one of the most successful men you have ever sat beside."

When Christian marriages are flourishing and experiencing the unity Christ is talking about, the world takes notice.

Readying himself for another assault from Mr. Alligator Shoes, Bob waited. But instead of an assault, he saw tears gathering in the man's eyes. The rest of his story began to unfold as he shared that just two weeks earlier he had arrived home from a trip and found a note from his wife that read: "Your daughters and I have left, and you will never see us again." For the next two hours the men talked about how real satisfaction and success are measured.

Finish well, and leave a legacy of faithfulness.

As we write, Virginia's father and mother are about to celebrate their 64th wedding anniversary. Unfortunately, Virginia's father has not been able to fully enter into their anniversary celebrations for many years, as he continues his decline with dementia. Virginia's mom lovingly cares for him, even though he is no longer able to contribute to household and personal routines. Dad is a retired Rear Admiral. He served with distinction in the Navy for over 35 years, during which time he was often deployed. During the Vietnam era, he was gone 32 of 36 months. During their time apart, Mom wrote to Dad every evening. At the same time, somewhere around the world, Dad would be doing the same thing. They numbered each letter, so that when the mail drop came at

sea every two weeks, Dad would be able to read the letters sequen-
tially and know if any were missing—and when the postman came
with the mail bonanza, Mom would know in what order to read
the letters from him as well. Virginia says that on those days when
the mail came, all the children knew not to disturb Mom. It was
like the locked door on their bedroom when Dad was home. Mom
and Dad were connecting even though thousands of miles separated them. When Virginia asked Mom how she managed to write
so faithfully while being a "single mom" to seven children, Mom
said, "It was the highlight of my day. It was the way your dad and
I stayed connected all those years."

After hearing this story at a conference, a woman whose husband was also out at sea for months at a time was moved to tears,
admitting that her husband had asked her to just email him each
day to let him know how she and the kids were doing, and she was
often "too busy."

Even though Dad no longer knows Mom's name, he is fully aware
that this woman is his sweetheart and he wants to hold her hand
and say "I love you" throughout the day. This sort of relationship
does not happen just by good intentions—it takes intentionality.

THE DELIGHT OF BEING A WITNESS TO THE WORLD

In what is known as the High Priestly Prayer, Jesus prays for
those left on earth as His witnesses to have . . . unity. If I were
thinking of one thing to ask for, I might ask for correct theology,
better witnessing skills, or generous giving—but Christ asks for
unity. Unity may be one of the most difficult things for us to model
as couples. Remember how we began this book? God said it is not
good to be alone, but Satan tries to do all he can to prevent community and unity. It is no secret that many couples are longing
for unity in their marriages but are finding only tolerance at best.

When Christian marriages are flourishing and experiencing the
unity Christ is talking about, the world takes notice.

Gary Thomas comments:

> In a society where relationships are discarded with
> a frightening regularity, Christians can command atten-
> tion simply by staying married. And when asked why, we
> can offer the platform of God's message of reconciliation,
> followed by an invitation: "Would you like to hear more
> about that good news of reconciliation?"
>
> In this sense, our marriages can be platforms for evan-
> gelism. They can draw people into a truth that points
> beyond this world into the next. Just by sticking it out in
> our marriages, we can build a monument to the principle
> and the practice of reconciliation.[29]

Some friends of ours have eight children. The parents didn't
become followers of Christ until after their children were born.
The husband became a follower of Christ first, followed by his
wife. Soon, all the children had seen what God had done in their
parents' lives and each of them made a personal decision for
Christ. Your story may not be as dramatic as this family's, but we
must not underestimate the effect a changed life can have on those
around us.

Your family and neighbors are watching! You can help them see
the power of Christ to bring life to a marriage and family.

> *"My prayer is not for them alone. I pray also for those who will*
> *believe in me through their message, that all of them may*
> *be one, Father, just as you are in me and I am in you. May*
> *they also be in us so that the world may believe that you have*
> *sent me."* —John 17:20–21

Our unity gives credibility to the power and reality of the
Gospel. When we as couples live lives of unity and intimacy before
a watching world, not only do we find joy ourselves—God uses us
to point others to the truth of the Gospel that is able to take sinful,
selfish human beings and lead them to dwell together in unity.

Is There Delight After Despair?

One of the questions we are most frequently asked in our counseling office is "Is there any hope for us?"

The answer is a resounding YES! God sent His Son to earth to live, die, and be resurrected so that we might have hope. Our hope ultimately is not in clever self-help books, or even gifted counselors, or couples "doing the work." Our hope is in the One who died to take our sins and give us His power so that we could be reconciled not only to Him but to each other.

> *Our unity gives credibility to the power and reality of the Gospel.*

A number of years ago, a couple came to a marriage conference, separated. I know it sounds odd, but they had signed up for the weekend and paid the non-refundable fees before they had separated. They figured that since the weekend was in a beautiful place, with meals included, they might as well show up and enjoy it, since they could certainly sleep in separate beds and just not talk to each other. As the weekend progressed, the two of them asked if they could talk to Virginia and me about how to divorce in a way that would not hurt their two daughters, ages 8 and 10. We told them we didn't really do that sort of counseling, but agreed to meet with them.

Fast forward eight years: Virginia and I are in Trinidad with our daughters, leading a family missions trip. I am sitting in the young church that our team had the privilege of helping to found in this Hindu community the year before. I was the preacher that morning. Our teammates Rich and Sue were leading the music. Do you know who they were? Yes, they were the couple we had met with 8 years earlier, and they were there in Trinidad with us, leading worship along with one of their daughters, while the other daughter stood among the Trinidadians in the congregation. Filled with joy, I thought to myself, "Isn't God good!" Rich had become a Christian; he and Sue had worked hard and were now reconciled and raising two teenage daughters in the ways of the Lord.

I don't know what your situation is, but there *is* hope.

Now to him who is able to do immeasurably more than all we ask or imagine, according to his power that is at work within us, to him be glory in the church and in Christ Jesus throughout all generations, for ever and ever! Amen.

—*Ephesians 3:20–21*

You see, the problem isn't that we expect too much from God, but that we don't have a clue how much God wants to give us if we will just trust Him and allow Him to bring healing and health to our marriages.

IN THE END, THE CHOICE IS OURS

When I was 20 years old, I was the skipper for Campus By the Sea, a camp on Santa Catalina Island. One day I was asked to pick up two men who were from a tree-trimming company. The owner of the company, Mr. Roseberry, was in his 60s, and his climber, Curley, was in his 20s. After picking them up, I realized the boat was low on gasoline, so I went to the fuel dock in the harbor. After refueling, I started the boat, but it was running really roughly. I did what many men do in such situations: I lifted the hatch and stared at the engine—but it didn't run any better. I then thought that if I pumped the throttle and gave it more gas, the engine might run better. What it did was explode.

I had failed to run the bilge blower, as I should have. There was also a gas leak that caused fumes that, had I run the bilge blower, would not have been an issue.

The boat exploded, sending Curley, who was on fire, about 10 feet in the air, and then into the bay. Mr. Roseberry was also on fire, and also shot up about 10 feet in the air, but when he came down, he landed on his back on the engine block. I was on fire as well. I lifted Mr. Roseberry out of the boat, and we all went to the hospital.

Curley and I got out the next day, but Mr. Roseberry stayed in the hospital for about 10 days. His burns were a bit more severe, but his long stay in the hospital was due to the significant injury he sustained to his back when he landed on the engine block.

> *We don't have a clue how much God wants to give us if we will just trust Him and allow Him to bring healing and health to our marriages.*

Mr. Roseberry lived for about another 15 years after the explosion. Every time I was with Mr. Roseberry and we met someone new, this is how he introduced me: "I would like you to meet Paul Friesen. He's the man who saved my life." And that was a true statement. I had picked him up out of a burning boat and carried him to safety.

There is another way he could have introduced me that would have also been true: "I'd like you to meet Paul Friesen. He's the jerk who almost killed me, and because of him, I have walked with excruciating pain in my back since the day of the explosion." Mr. Roseberry gave me a gift that I will remember until my final breath. He made me a hero instead of a villain. Same situation, different heart.

You have read a lot of stories and considered a lot of scriptural truth, but at the end of the day it will come down to your heart. Are you for each other? Do you want to make one another heroes, or would you really prefer painting each other as villains? Have a heart to make the other a hero, and your spouse will likely grow to be more of one. Have a heart to make your spouse a villain, and he or she may well become just that.

The choice is up to you.

When we put our spouse's needs above our own,
not only will they feel loved,
but it will propel our marriage towards greater intimacy.

Reminders

☑ It is counterintuitive to put others' needs ahead of our own.

☑ Couples that are "other-focused" tend to be much more alive than those that focus on themselves.

☑ When we attempt to appreciate the communication style of our spouse, our marriage is strengthened.

☑ When we seek to please our spouse sexually rather than simply thinking of ourselves, our experience is much richer.

☑ Forgiveness is the oil that keeps marriages running smoothly.

☑ There is always hope for marital renewal. It is never too late to do the right thing.

☑ When we live in unity as a couple, we are a witness to the world of the power of the Gospel.

☑ The choice is ours as to how we respond to each other, making each other heroes or villains.

For Couples

Questions

1. Reflect on when your marriage was the closest to experiencing intimacy in every dimension most fully. What was it that contributed to that time?

2. Each of you describe the couple that most clearly exemplifies what you believe is God's design for marriage. What is it that you see in them that you would like to be a characteristic of your own marriage?

APPlication

- Each of you write a note or post-it to each other and "hide" it so they will find it during the day. On the note, finish the sentence "I delight in being married to you because _____."

- Get child care if you need it and go out for a special evening to celebrate God's gift of marriage and each other.

For Groups

1. Read John 17:20–27. Why do you think Jesus' only request for His followers is unity?

2. Why is unity among believers, families, and couples such a powerful witness?

3. Share one take-away from this book that you believe will lead to greater unity in your marriage.

4. Share stories of couples you know that fully delight in each other.

5. Share personally how your spouse, in putting your needs ahead of his or her own, has brought delight to your marriage.

6. Go around the room and each share a positive trait you see in your spouse.

7. Pray for each other, asking God to strengthen your marriages and use them as a witness to the world.

Notes

Chapter 1   Care for the one you love.

1. Farrar, Steve. *Point Man: How a Man Can Lead His Family*. Multnomah Books, 2003. (or Random House Digital, 2009)

Chapter 2   Have realistic expectations.

2. Kreider, Rose M., and Fields, Jason M. *Number, Timing, and Duration of Marriages and Divorces: 1996*. Current Population Reports, P70-80, US Census Bureau, 2001, p. 18.
    http://www.census.gov/prod/2002pubs/p70-80.pdf accessed 4/6/2013.

3. US Census Bureau. *Statistical Abstract of the United States: 2012*. Section 2: Births, Deaths, Marriages, and Divorces, Table 132, p. 97.
    http://www.census.gov/prod/2011pubs/12statab/vitstat.pdf accessed 4/6/2013.

4. Thomas, Gary. *Sacred Marriage*. Zondervan, 2000, pp. 186–187.

Chapter 3   Appreciate your differences.

5. Allender, Dan. *Intimate Allies*. Tyndale House, 1995, p. 33.

6. Allender, p. 19.

7. Rainey, Dennis and Barbara. *Building Your Mate's Self-Esteem*. Focus on the Family, 1986, p. 225.

8. Keirsey, David, and Bates, Marilyn. *Please Understand Me: Character & Temperament Types*. Gnosology Books / Prometheus Nemesis, 1984.

Chapter 4   Realize the enemy is not your spouse.

9. Mason, Mike. *The Mystery of Marriage*. Multnomah Press, 1985, p. 91.

10. Thomas, p. 23.

11. Charen, Mona. "Sticking It Out, Happily Ever After." *Baltimore Sun*, July 22, 2002.

12. Crabb, Larry. *The Marriage Builder*. Zondervan, 1982, p. 119.

13. Graham, Ruth Bell. *It's My Turn*. Revell, 1982, p. 74.

14. Crabb, p. 123.

Chapter 5   Keep marriage your priority.

Chapter 6   Be intentional in pursuing each other.

15. Chapman, Gary. *The Five Love Languages: How to Express Heartfelt Commitment to Your Mate*. Northfield Publishing, 1992.

Chapter 7   Give each other love and respect.

16.   Crabb, p. 119.

17.   Hunt, Susan. *The True Woman: The Beauty and Strength of a Godly Woman.* Crossway, 1997, pp. 218, 223.

18.   Heald, Cynthia. *Loving Your Husband: Building an Intimate Marriage in a Fallen World.* NavPress, 1989, pp. 50–51.

Chapter 8   Experience the joy in sacrificial love.

19.   Keller, Timothy. *The Meaning of Marriage: Facing the Complexities of Commitment with the Wisdom of God.* Dutton, 2011, p. 100.

Chapter 9   Find new life through forgiveness.

20.   Regan, Brian. "Eye Doctor" (comedy routine). *http://www.youtube.com/watch?v=v8GMFkc3iSA* (video), 0:00–0:24, accessed 4/6/2013. Also on his DVD *I Walked on the Moon* (2004), track 9.

21.   ten Boom, Corrie. *Tramp for the Lord.* Revell / Christian Literature Crusade, 1974, ch. 33.

22.   Banschick, Mark, M.D., *The Intelligent Divorce* (blog). February 6, 2012. *http://www.psychologytoday.com/blog/the-intelligent-divorce/201202/the-high-failure-rate-second-and-third-marriages/* accessed 4/6/2013.

23.   Nixon, Richard Milhous. Farewell speech to White House staff. August 9, 1974. Quoted in Wooten, James T., "Tears at Parting: Ex-President Warns Against Bitterness and Revenge." *New York Times,* August 10, 1974, p. 1; full text of speech on p. 4. See also *http://www.youtube.com/watch?v=1Ff1jxlVPEQ* (video), 0:13–0:25, accessed 4/6/2013.

24.   Freud, Sigmund. *Civilization and Its Discontents.* 1930, Chapter V, footnote 1.

25.   Smedes, Lewis, B. *Forgive and Forget: Healing the Hurts We Don't Deserve.* HarperCollins, 1984, 1996, p. 29.

26.   MacDonald, Gail. *Keep Climbing: Turning the Challenges of Life into Adventures of the Spirit.* Tyndale House, 1989, p. 80.

27.   Sittser, Gerald. *A Grace Disguised: How the Soul Grows through Loss.* Zondervan, 1995, pp. 127, 128.

Chapter 10   Delight in each other.

28.   *http://espn.go.com/blog/afceast/post/_/id/14930/tom-brady-still-listens-to-qb-whisperer/* accessed 4/6/2013.

29.   Thomas, p. 37.

About the Authors

Drs. Paul and Virginia Friesen were married in 1976 and are the parents of three young women, two of whom are now married to wonderful, Godly men. They have been involved in Family Ministries for over 35 years through family camps, church staff positions, speaking, consulting, and writing. In 2003, they founded Home Improvement Ministries (www.HIMweb.org), a non-profit organization dedicated to equipping individuals and churches to better encourage marriages and families in living out God's design for healthy relationships. Paul and Virginia both have Doctorates in Marriage and Family Therapy from Gordon-Conwell Theological Seminary.

As the lead resource couple at Home Improvement Ministries, the Friesens regularly speak at marriage, men's, and women's conferences in the US and internationally, as well as local family and parenting seminars, and have an ongoing ministry with several professional athletic teams. The Friesens have authored ten books and produced numerous DVDs on parenting and marriage.

Paul and Virginia's greatest joy in life is knowing that their children are walking in the Truth.

Other resources available from Home Improvement Ministries:

Parenting

Raising a Trailblazer, Virginia Friesen. (book)
Parenting by Design, Paul and Virginia Friesen.
(DVD series, with study guide)
The Father's Heart, Paul and Virginia Friesen.
(DVD series, with study guide)

Dating and Engagement

Letters to My Daughters, Paul Friesen. (book)
Letters to My Daughters Discussion Guide, Paul Friesen. (study guide)
Before You Save the Date, Paul Friesen. (book)
So You Want to Marry My Daughter?, Paul Friesen. (book)
Engagement Matters, Paul and Virginia Friesen. (study guide)

Marriage

Restoring the Fallen, Earl and Sandy Wilson, Paul and Virginia
Friesen, Larry and Nancy Paulson. (book)
Marriage, Culture, and Scripture, Paul and Virginia Friesen. (book)
In Our Image, Paul and Virginia Friesen. (study guide)
Jesus on Marriage, Paul and Virginia Friesen. (study guide)
Recapturing Eden, Paul and Virginia Friesen.
(DVD series, with study guide)
Created in God's Image, Paul and Virginia Friesen.
(DVD series, with study guide)

Discipleship

Gospel Revolution, Gabriel Garcia. (book)

For more information about Home Improvement Ministries or to order
any of our products, please contact us:

Call: 781-275-6473

Email: info@himweb.org

Write: Home Improvement Ministries
213 Burlington Road, Suite 101-B
Bedford, MA 01730 USA

Online: www.HIMweb.org/books (for the online bookstore)
www.HIMweb.org/speak (to book speakers).
www.HIMweb.org/fb   (to reach us on Facebook)